BEAUTY FOODS

CAROLINE ARTISS

BEAUTY FOODS

65 nutritious and delicious
recipes that make you shine
from the inside out

photography by Ed Anderson

RYLAND PETERS & SMALL
LONDON • NEW YORK

Senior designer Megan Smith
Commissioning editor Stephanie Milner
Head of Production Patricia Harrington
Art director Leslie Harrington
Editorial director Julia Charles
Publisher Cindy Richards

Food stylist George Dolese
Food stylist's assistant Elisabet der Nederlanden
Prop stylist Emma Star Jensen

Indexer Vanessa Bird

First published in 2016 by
Ryland Peters & Small
20–21 Jockey's Fields, London
WC1R 4BW and
341 E 116th St,
New York NY 10029
www.rylandpeters.com

10 9 8 7 6 5 4 3 2 1

ISBN: 978-1-84975-768-3

Printed in China

A CIP record for this book is available
from the British Library. US Library
of Congress Cataloging-in-Publication
Data has been applied for.

Notes
• Both British (Metric) and
American (Imperial plus US cups)
measurements are included in these
recipes for convenience; however
it is important to work with one set
of measurements and not alternate
between the two within a recipe.
• All spoon measurements are
level unless otherwise specified.
• All eggs are medium (UK) or large
(US), unless specified as large, in
which case US extra-large should
be used.
• Ovens should be preheated
to the specified temperatures.

We recommend using an oven
thermometer. If using a fan-assisted
oven, adjust temperatures according
to the manufacturer's instructions.
• When a recipe calls for the grated
zest of citrus fruit, buy unwaxed fruit
and wash well before using. If you
can only find treated fruit, scrub well
in warm soapy water before using.

Disclaimer
The views expressed in this book
are those of the author but they are
general views only and readers
are urged to consult a relevant and
qualified specialist or physician for
individual advice before beginning
any dietary regimen.

Contents

Introduction

I think from a young age I knew food was my path in life, I trained as a chef when I was 15 years old and I've been in the food world ever since. This first cookbook of mine is very close to my heart as it is dedicated to my mother who sadly passed away last year while I was in the middle of writing it. My mother was a top beautician who had her own successful beauty clinic called Hibiscus in Stoke Poges, England. Beauty was her passion in life and she had the healing hands and knowledge to help many people look their absolute best. My sisters, brother and I grew up with the importance of taking care of our skin, hair, teeth and health drilled into us. My mother always believed in the more natural beauty regimes and treatments. The house was filled with the scents of lavender, tea tree and peppermint from her aromatherapy. Her Chinese-Malaysian heritage taught me so much about using food to heal certain ailments and for keeping us healthy and looking good. If we were ever sick or unwell, the ginger root would be whipped out and made into a ginger, honey and lemon tea, or a pot of chicken soup would be on the stove, which my mother told me would also keep me looking young. The cupboards were full of strange dried mushrooms and the freezer full of small dried fish which were to be used in soups and broths, stir fries and a whole assortment of dishes.

This all led me (alongside my love for food) to be more conscious of what I was eating in combination with a good daily skincare regime. As well as working as a chef, I studied for a food nutrition diploma as I was so fascinated by how the food we eat plays such a crucial part in our health, and how different ingredients play different roles in nourishing our bodies and minds.

My mother's knowledge of the beauty field and my love for food and nutrition lead to this book being created. One thing that had the biggest impact on me when writing this book was how my mother never liked to take artificial supplements, she always said if we eat a good enough diet we get all the nutrients we need. I too believe that if we eat healthily we can nourish our bodies with everything they need by eating the right foods. I developed the recipes in this book using a good mixture of ingredients available at your local supermarket, and some which have specific superfood qualities that you'll most likely find at a health food store. I'm a working single mother so budget has always been something I have to think about and I didn't want my recipes to break the bank.

My advice for using this book as part of your beauty regime is to pick a couple of recipes from each category of skin, hair and nails, digestion and so on, to get a well-balanced, all-over beauty diet. Thank you for buying this book and for using my recipes. I truly hope you enjoy making these recipes and that they help you shine from the inside out.

HOW TO USE THIS BOOK

At the side of each recipe title you'll find an icon indicating that it will benefit your:

- **S**   SKIN
- **H**   HAIR AND NAILS
- **E**   EYES
- **M**   MUSCLES
- **D**   DIGESTION
- **B**   BONES AND TEETH

Beauty Foods

SKIN

The largest organ of the body; there is a wealth of research that identifies why certain nutrients are essential for keeping our skin looking healthy. All these nutrients can be found in natural foods and should be added to your plate for beauty.

Healthy skin needs fat. People who cut out all fats from their diets to encourage weight-loss will most likely suffer with dry, aged skin. Essential fatty acids like omega-3 and omega-6 help build cell membranes that keep the skin's natural oil barrier in tact, ensuring soft, plump skin. Include ingredients with good fat content, such as *coconut, olive* and *algae oil, oily fish,* avocados, seaweed, *chia seeds, flaxseeds/linseeds* and nuts.

Antioxidants protect the skin. We've all heard of antioxidants, but what do they actually do? Well, they limit the production of free radicals, which can damage skin cells and lead to signs of early aging. They also help protect the skin from the sun's harmful UV rays. There are many skincare products that contain added antioxidants and vitamins, but I say remember to get them straight from the source and eat them up. Antioxidants have a great anti-inflammatory effect and reducing inflammation promotes a more even skin tone, keeping acne and wrinkles at bay. Good sources of antioxidants to stock up on include *black beans, black rice, green tea, dark/bittersweet chocolate, moringa powder, red grapes, baobab fruit powder, spinach, kale, artichokes* and *broccoli,* and, of course, *berries.* Rather than just eating bucket-loads of blueberries to get all your antioxidants, it is far more beneficial to eat a whole range of the foods mentioned above and in the following pages. It's really important to take a balanced approach to getting all the

nutritional value from ingredients that your skin needs through your diet. I believe that is why the world is blessed with such a huge variety of foods, so that we can try different flavour combinations and still find everything we need in nature to keep our bodies feeling healthy and looking great.

Vitamins A, C and E reduce fine lines and wrinkles. Vitamin A is transformed into retinol in the body, which is essential for clear skin. Studies have shown that retinol helps to keep the skin firm by increasing the skin's collagen production, creating healthy cells and increasing skin support substances, such as ceramides. Great sources of vitamin A are all the orange-coloured vegetables, like *butternut squash, carrots* and *sweet potatoes,* as well as *beetroot/beet tops, green beans, spinach, dark cabbage* and *kale.*

Vitamin C is essential in the production of scar tissue, blood vessels and cartilage – it is also a powerful antioxidant and helps promote collagen production. Great sources to stock up on are *apples, apricots, citrus fruit, pears, kiwi, guava, papaya* and *mango, yellow, orange* or *red (bell) peppers, dark green leafy vegetables, cauliflower, Brussels sprouts, radishes* and *tomatoes* to name just a few!

Vitamin E is a potent antioxidant that helps protect the skin from sun damage. It cannot be produced by the body, so we need to make sure we eat enough to replenish the body's store. Good sources (that you can find easily without having to buy supplements) are *tofu, almonds, hazelnuts, sunflower, pumpkin* and *sesame seeds, avocados, oily fish,* like *salmon, trout* and *herring, prawns/ shrimp* and *swordfish.* It is also present in *spinach, kale* and *turnip greens,* as well as *wheatgerm, olive, grapeseed* and *sunflower oils.*

INGREDIENT	CONTENT	BEAUTY BENEFIT
Açai berries	Calcium, fibre, phytochemicals, protein, vitamin A	This Amazonian blueish-purple berry is hailed for its potent level of antioxidant vitamins and phytochemicals that prevent premature aging.
Agave syrup	Fibre, iron, selenium, vitamins A, C, E and K	A natural sweetener, with a lower glycemic index (GI) than many other sugar sources. Iron supports oxygen transportation around the body and with it helps the skin to absorb nutrients from other sources.
Almonds	Calcium, copper, fibre, folate, iron, manganese, omega-3 and 6, protein, riboflavin, vitamin E	Omega-3 and omega-6 are good fats that help the skin stay soft and supple. Vitamin E protects against harmful free radicals and sun damage.
Avocados	Calcium, fibre, iron, oleic acid, protein, vitamins A, C, E and K	Vitamin E is a fat-soluble vitamin, which helps protect the skin from harmful oxidative damage to cells, and oleic acid is known for speeding up cell regeneration, healing wounds and reducing inflammation.
Basil	Manganese, omega-3, omega-6, vitamins A, C and K	The combination of manganese and vitamin K in basil is anti-bacterial and anti-fungal. It helps clear skin infections and keep skin pimple-free.
Beetroot/beets	Fibre, folate, manganese, omega-6, potassium, vitamins C	The high levels of folate in beetroot/beets stimulate the production and repair of skins cells, which helps to prevent premature aging.
Blueberries	Fibre, manganese, phytochemicals, vitamins C and K	Antioxidant-rich and a great source of anthocyanins (giving the blue pigmentation), blueberries help fight free-radical damage to cells, which keeps skin firm. The vitamin C helps to produce collagen for plump skin.
Brazil nuts	Calcium, copper, magnesium, omega-6, selenium, thiamin, vitamin E	Native to South America, these tasty nuts are full of skin-boosting goodness. Selenium helps skin to glow by speeding up the cell turnover process and vitamin E helps to protect skin from harmful UV rays.
Brussels sprouts	Omega-3, omega-6, potassium, vitamins C and K	Brussels sprouts contain high levels of nutrients, antioxidants and vitamin C, which protect skin from free radicals and produce collagen.
Chillies/chiles	Capsaicin, iron, manganese, omega-6, potassium, vitamins A, B6, C and K	The active ingredient capsaicin is a thermogenic, meaning it helps the body burn fat through metabolic processes. Capsaicin is also known to help protect skin from the sun's harmful UV rays.
Cinnamon	Calcium, iron, manganese	Used for its medicinal purposes for centuries in Asian cultures, cinnamon can help increase blood flow to the skin surface giving plumper, younger looking skin. It can also increase collagen production and helps clear skin conditions with its anti-bacterial and anti-fungal properties.
Coconut	Copper, fibre, folate, iron, manganese, omega-6, protein, vitamins B1 (thiamin) and C	Coconut flesh is low in carbohydrates and high in both fibre and medium-chain saturated fats, which keep skin hydrated and moist. It is also a plant-based protein that can be harnessed for energy.
Coconut oil	Omega-6, vitamin E	Coconut oil can be consumed orally as well as applied topically on the skin. Its fats are a good source of fuel and help to keep skin soft. The omega-6 fatty acids have disinfectant and anti-microbial properties that help to protect the skin, while the vitamin E content repairs damaged skin.
Coconut palm sugar	Carbohydrate sugars	Coconut palm sugar is a natural sugar made from the sap of the coconut plant. It has a lower glycemic index (GI) than other sugars and is more nutritious – a great sweet substitute for refined white sugar.
Cranberries	Fibre, manganese, phytochemicals, vitamins E and K	Cranberries are packed full of antioxidants that help prevent oxidation damage of cells from free radicals, and the large amounts of polyphenols and flavonoids help to repair skin damage and prevent infection.
Goji berries	Calcium, copper, iron, phytochemicals, potassium, selenium, vitamins A and C	Goji berries originate form China and are known for their powerful anti-aging effect. The high levels of antioxidants contained within them helps to protect the skin cells from damage and therefore premature aging.

INGREDIENT	CONTENT	BEAUTY BENEFIT
Green vegetables	Fibre	We need plenty of green vegetables in our diet every day to help provide essential minerals and vitamins and to provide fibre to aid digestion and keep moving the waste out of our bodies and away from the skin surface.
Hazelnuts	Copper, fibre, folate, omega-3, omega-6, manganese, protein, vitamins B1 (thiamin), B6, C, E, K	The vitamin E in the hazelnuts, along with other good fats, helps to keep the skin hydrated and plump, soft and supple, reducing fine lines.
Hemp seeds	Iron, magnesium, omega-3, omega-6, protein, zinc	A great source of essential fatty acids, which are needed to support healthy cells and brain and nerve functions. The body cannot make its own fatty acids so we need good sources from our diet. They are known to be very good for dry skin conditions, acne and even varicose veins.
Honey	Carbohydrate sugars, iron, manganese	Honey has a wealth of skin friendly antioxidants and antibacterial compounds and enzymes. These help keep the skin clean and clear and honey can also be used to heal wounds. Raw honey is the best as it contains active phytonutrient enzymes which have potent benefits.
Lemongrass	Folate, iron, manganese, potassium	Lemongrass can help keep skin clean and clear with its host of antiseptic, antibacterial and anti-microbial properties, helping to ward off infection. Like lemon, it is also an astringent, which means it can help minimize pores, and is a natural mosquito repellant.
Lemons and limes	Citric acid, vitamins A and C	Lemons and limes are good sources of vitamins C and A that help protect skin cells from damage, keeping skin looking younger. The antibacterial, astringent properties of citric acid also helps to reduce bacteria on the skin surface and can be used topically to remove dead skin cells.
Matcha green tea	Chlorophyll, epigallocatechin gallate, iron, protein, vitamin A	Green tea is hailed for its powerful antioxidant properties and also the high level of chlorophyll (the green colour of the plant) that help the body detoxify and get rid of harmful toxins, which is crucial for clear and healthy skin. Green tea contains epigallocatechin gallate (EGCG), an antioxidant which is known to slow down the degeneration of skin cells.
Oranges	Calcium, fibre, folate, phytonutrients, potassium, vitamins A and C	Oranges are a great source of vitamin C, an antioxidant that protects skin cells from free radical damage, reduces inflammation and builds a strong immune system. Vitamin C plays a key role in the formation of collagen which is the support system of our skin.
Pistachios	Calcium, copper, fibre, iron, omega-3, omega-6, manganese, phosphorus, potassium, protein, selenium, vitamins A, B6, C, E, K	Pistachios have a high concentration of vitamin E which is excellent for keeping skin looking young. Vitamin E improves the skin's elasticity, while the vitamin C protects the skin cells from damage.
Pomegranate	Copper, ellagic acid, fibre, folate, omega-6, potassium, protein, vitamins B6, C, E and K	Pomegranates are an anti-aging powerhouse. With high levels of antioxidants to fight the free radicals and protect and nourish skin cells, they also contain anti-aging compounds that stimulate cell regeneration.
Raw sugar	Glucose	Raw sugar is a great natural sweetener. It hasn't been refined so still contains vitamins and minerals unlike white refined sugar which has no nutritional value. It can be used topically as an exfoliant body scrub and it is great for getting rid of dead skin cells.
Salmon	Omega-3, omega-6, phosphorus, protein, selenium, vitamins B6, B12 and C	Salmon is rich in omega-3 fatty acids which help to reduce inflammation and keep skin membrane layers hydrated, which in turn helps to keep out toxins and makes skin look plump and young.
Tomatoes	Lypocene, potassium, vitamins A, C and K	Lypocene is a natural plant chemical carotenoid that gives tomatoes their red pigmentation. It has antioxidant properties that protect the skin from harmful UV rays, and helps support skin structure by aiding the production of collagen.

HAIR AND NAILS

Always wanted thick, strong, shiny, luscious locks? Rather than buying every new hair product under the sun, it's time to get into the kitchen.

Hair follicles are the fastest growing cells in the body, but they are also the cells that lose out if the body needs the nutrients that feed them somewhere else more important to general health. The body is incredibly clever like that, it prioritizes vitamins and minerals to be used to help the most important functions in the body, like our hearts and vital organs, before replenishing resources for hair, nails and other body parts. Sadly our hair is not considered essential for our survival, although I have some friends who beg to differ. Serious hair loss can be caused by a deficiency in nutrients, a bad diet, stress and also hereditary genes.

Hair and nails are made from protein fibres. Hair strands consist of 90 per cent protein, so they need plenty of protein to keep growing. If you don't eat enough protein-rich foods, your body will cut off the supply to hair follicles and use the protein where it is needed for more important bodily functions. This not only stops growth but also makes hair and nails dry and brittle. Plant-based proteins such as *legumes, soy products, quinoa, lentils* and *nuts*, as well as animal products (*meat, fish, cheese* and *eggs*) should be eaten regularly.

Iron is essential for strong hair and nails. It produces red blood cells which carry oxygen and nutrients to all of our cells. A good source of iron is *red meat*, which contains ferritin, a type of stored iron that helps the body produce hair-cell proteins. Some *fish* and *scallops* are also good sources. If you're a vegetarian or vegan, then good plant sources of iron are *apricots, soy* products, *kidney beans, chickpeas, pinto beans, whole grains* like amaranth, and *green leafy veggies.* It's important to eat the foods high in iron with foods that are also high in vitamin C, which enhances the absorption of iron and provides a source of antioxidants that nourish hair. Try eating a steak for the iron with a tomato salad for the vitamin C. It's about getting the balance right. *Garlic* is also high in vitamin C so I like to add it to dressings.

Biotin strengthens hair and nails. This B-vitamin helps metabolize carbohydrates and amino acids, which are the building blocks of protein. The body can't store this vitamin so we need to make sure we regularly include good sources, such as *eggs, Swiss chard, carrots, almonds, walnuts, onions, strawberries, raspberries, halibut, cucumber, cauliflower, tahini, milk* and *nut milks* in our diets.

Omega-3 fatty acids keep hair shiny and hydrated. Good sources include *egg yolks, oily fish* like *salmon, sardines* and *mackerel,* plus *flaxseeds/linseeds, chia seeds* and *hemp seeds* have good levels of plant-based omega-3s.

Vitamin D helps keep hair follicles strong. It also aids the absorption of calcium which encourages nail growth. Good sources of vitamin D include *oily fish,* mushrooms (*Portobello, maitake, morel*), *tofu, soy yogurt, caviar, pork, eggs* and don't forget sunshine! Add to these calcium-rich foods for double the dosage of goodness. Include *dairy* products, *ghee, almond* and *soy milks, black strap molasses, spinach, seaweed, sardines, white* and *black-eyed beans, figs, pak choi/bok choy, kale, oranges, turnip greens* and *nuts.*

Vitamin A helps the scalp to produce oils to keep it soft and not dry or flaky. Ingredients packed with vitamin A include *spirulina, sweet potatoes, squashes, carrots* and most other *orange veggies!* I created the recipes for hair and nails with a matrix of hair goodness in mind, so that you can create a well-balanced mix of essential nutrients.

INGREDIENT	CONTENT	BEAUTY BENEFIT
Black salsify root	Calcium, iron, fibre, magnesium, manganese, phosphorus, potassium, vitamins B6 and C	Black salsify root contains an abundance of healthy hair nutrients. Iron helps carry oxygen to the hair cells and copper helps with hair growth and strengthening hair strands.
Bones (bone broth)	Calcium, collagen, glycine, protein	Bone broth is an excellent source of cooked collagen, which turns to gelatin. Collagen is essential for keeping the skin structure firm, while gelatin can help ease gut issues and improve digestion.
Broccoli	Beta-carotene, calcium, fibre, folate, glucoraphanin, iron, manganese, phosphorus, potassium, vitamins A, B6, C, E, K	The calcium in broccoli strengthens hair follicles for shiny locks. Broccoli also contains a compound called glucoraphanin, which helps regenerate skin damaged by harmful UV rays.
Cabbage	Keratin, sulphur, silicone, vitamins A, B6, C, E and K	Cabbage contains sulphur, which helps our bodies to produce a protein called keratin which is essential for healthy hair, nails and skin.
Cauliflower	Fibre, folate, manganese, phosphorus, potassium, sulphur, silicone, vitamins A, B6, C, E and K	The presence of sulphur and silicone in cauliflower helps promote hair growth and healthy skin. As with cabbage, the sulphur helps keep hair strong with some elasticity –a lack of sulphur can lead to dry, brittle hair.
Enoki mushrooms	Copper, iron, phytochemicals, vitamin B3 (niacin)	Niacin, also known as vitamin B3 is a very important nutrient for hair growth. Its specific function is to help rebuild DNA in damaged hair and to help promote new growth in hair cells. Enoki mushrooms are also a low-carbohydrate vegetable.
Kidney beans	Fibre, folate, iron, manganese, protein, vitamin B7 (biotin), zinc	Kidney beans are great for maintaining healthy hair as they contain many essential nutrients, including iron, zinc and biotin, plus proteins that promote new cell growth.
Moringa powder	Amino acids, calcium, iron, magnesium, omega-3, potassium, vitamins A, C, E and K	Moringa powder promotes hair growth through the absorption of vitamins and potassium, while the high levels of antioxidants keep skin looking younger and the fatty acids keep the skin hydrated and plump.
Scallops	Amino acids, cystine, magnesium, potassium, selenium, vitamin B12	Scallops are packed full of healthy hair nutrients. One of them being cystine, which is a sulphur containing amino acids that promotes healthy skin, hair, bones and connective tissues.
Sesame seeds	Calcium, copper, fibre, iron, manganese, magnesium, phosphorus, protein, vitamin B6, zinc	Sesame seeds are an excellent source of copper, which is essential for hair growth and is often added to commercial hair growth products. Copper is also responsible for the pigmentation of hair – black sesame seeds in particular have been known to keep grey hairs at bay.
Strawberries	Fibre, manganese, salicylic acid, vitamins B7 (biotin), C and K	Strawberries are a great source of antioxidants that help protect skin from UV-sun damage. The salicylic acid in them helps keep skin clear, and when used topically in face masks it can also help clear dead skin and impurities.
Swiss chard	Vitamins A, B7 (biotin), C, K	Swiss chard is one of the best natural sources of biotin, which is an essential nutrient for hair growth. Biotin, also known as vitamin H or B7, aids metabolism and processes energy. It is recommended for strengthening hair and aids the protein structure of keratin.
Turmeric	Curcumin, manganese, vitamin B7 (biotin)	Turmeric has been used for medicinal purposes for centuries in India. It has antiseptic and antibacterial properties, which can help with skin conditions like acne and pimples and also scalp conditions like dandruff. It can detoxify the liver, ridding toxins and keeping skin clear and bright.
Yeast	Amino acids, fibre, folate, iron, phosphorus	Yeast is good for hydration of the skin and so is excellent for scalp condition. Its antioxidant level gives good cell-regenerating properties that are used in anti-aging skin and haircare products.

EYES

The last 20 years or so has brought with it a wealth of research that links diet and nutrition with a decreased risk of eye-related health problems. I'm so grateful that I have good eyesight, as I couldn't imagine life without it. Eating certain foods that contain nutrients that scientists call 'eye-friendly' can help to keep your eyes bright and sparkly, so start with your diet and include these essential beauty foods.

The eyes are spectacular – a complex globe of lenses, corneas, pupils and protective layers that combine to capture images that are sent to our brains in nano-seconds. There are tiny arteries around the eyes that also need to be taken care of. Eye function is reduced with age but you can take steps to keep them healthy and looking good.

Beta-carotene is one of the best eye-friendly nutrients. It is found in all the orange-coloured vegetables: *carrots, butternut squash, sweet potatoes,* just think orange! It's a type of vitamin A which promotes eye health and helps the eye retina function properly. Eat plenty of foods that contain this super-nutrient.

Vitamin C is critical to eye health. Studies have shown that your eyes need a relatively high level of vitamin C in order to function properly. And consuming enough antioxidant-filled foods can help prevent or delay cataracts. Good sources of vitamin C include *berries* and *citrus fruit, tomatoes* and *red (bell) peppers.*

Antioxidants, such as lutein and zeaxanthin, which lower the risk of cataracts, can be found in *leafy green vegetables* and *egg yolks. Spinach,* which is also packed full of carotenoids, is the antioxidant that promotes healthy eyes and prevents macular degeneration, the leading cause of blindness in older people.

There are high levels of zinc in the eye. Zinc is an essential trace mineral that helps protect the eye from light, so you should take every opportunity you can to feast on good sources of zinc, including *kidney beans, chickpeas, pinto beans, scallops, oysters, whole grains, red meat* and *poultry.*

Vitamin E, DHA fatty acids and omega-3s are essential for retinal function. Vitamin E is thought to protect the cells in the eyes from free-radical damage, while DHA fatty acids and omega-3s are important for visual development, cell regeneration and good vision. Great natural sources of all three of these nutrients are *anchovies, salmon, trout, mackerel, tuna, chia seeds* and *flaxseeds/linseeds.*

INGREDIENT	CONTENT	BEAUTY BENEFIT
Algae oil	DHA fatty acids, omega-3	Algae oil is a great vegetarian source of DHAs and other essential fatty acids found largely in fish sources. Said to help reduce inflammatory conditions, they help improve memory and vision, heart and brain health.
Beetroot/beet green tops	calcium, copper, fibre, iron, magnesium, omega-3, omega-6, potassium, protein, manganese, vitamins A, B6, C and K	A highly nutritious and versatile leafy green vegetable, low in fat and high in vitamins, fibre, minerals and antioxidants. The high levels of vitamin K work with the calcium to promote good bone health and encourage light-filtering functions for the eyes.
Butternut squash	Carotene, fibre, lutein, vitamins A, B6, C and E, zeaxanthin	Antioxidants zeaxanthin and lutein are especially good for protecting your vision, preventing age-related macular degeneration and dry eyes.
Carrots	Carotene, fibre, potassium, vitamins A, B7 (biotin), C and K	Carrots are a great source of beta-carotene, which provides the orange colour. It's a form of vitamin A, essential for good vision and retina function.
Dark leafy greens	Beta-carotene, calcium, fibre, phytonutrients	Dark leafy green veggies, like kale, Swiss chard and spinach are excellent for all-round beauty as they contain so much goodness that feeds and nourishes every part of our bodies. From antioxidants to fight wrinkles, to iron to help our hair shine, beta-carotene to keep our eyes sparkling, fibre to aid our digestion for clearer skin, calcium for strong bones, the list goes on... eat plenty of leafy greens to keep yourself beautiful inside and out.
Egg yolks	Calcium, carotenoids, folate, iron, omega-3, omega-6, phosphorus, protein, selenium, vitamins A, B2 (riboflavin), B5 (pantothenic acid), B6, B12, D and E, zinc	Egg yolks are packed full of goodness but most importantly contain essential fatty acids and fat-soluble vitamins. The omega-3s are needed for proper brain and eye retina functions. The omega-6s are essential for healthy skin, hair, libido, reproductive system and growth.
Grapefruit	Fibre, lycopene, vitamins A and C	Lycopene, found in grapefruit, can diminish the appearance of dark circles around the eyes. Rich in skin healthy antioxidants and vitamin C, grapefruit can help produce collagen. The high-water content of the fruit helps keep the skin's outer layer hydrated so less wrinkles can form.
Kale	Calcium, carotenoids, copper, potassium, manganese, vitamins A and C	Kale is a great plant-based source of calcium and also vitamin K, which helps the body know where to use the calcium. Carotenoids significantly reduce the risk of age-related eye diseases.
Papaya	Beta-carotene, fibre, folate, lutein, vitamins A and C, zeaxanthin	Papaya is a great source of vitamins A, C and E, as well as having anti-inflammatory properties and a good dose of fibre for keeping you regular. Vitamin A limits the degeneration of eyesight.
Raspberries	Biotin, ellagic acid, fibre, manganese, vitamins A, C and K	Ellagic acid is a phytochemical that is found to be anti-carcinogenic and the high levels of antioxidants in raspberries helps protect our skin and cells from damage, while vitamin A is transformed into carotene for eyes.
Seaweed and kelp	Calcium, DHA fatty acids, magnesium, vitamin A	Marine extracts help hair to rebuild itself and stay shiny and strong, while vitamin A clears up the cellular debris that accumulates in eyes.
Spinach	Calcium, carotenoids, folate, iron, nitrates, vitamins A, C and K	Rich in carotenoids for vision and antioxidants and vitamins that help boost skin health, spinach also contains high levels of iron and essential minerals to keep blood cells healthy.
Sweet potatoes	Anthocyanin, beta-carotene, carotene, copper, fibre, potassium, manganese, vitamins A, B5 (pantothenic acid) and B6	Sweet potatoes are a great source of vitamin A which is essential for keeping the surface of the eye, the cornea, healthy. Sweet potatoes are also naturally high in beta-carotene, which is anti-inflammatory and one of the most effective forms of pro-vitamin A carotenoids.
Tuna	DHA fatty acids, iron, magnesium, phosphorus, potassium, protein, selenium, vitamins B3 (niacin), B6 and B12, zinc	Tuna is a great source of selenium which is needed to support elastin for firm and tight skin. DHA fatty acids are the primary oil in fish and it is linked with helping prevent age-related macular degeneration.

MUSCLES

We all know that working out and keeping fit is essential to keeping our muscles toned and strong. But did you know that feeding your muscles the right foods helps them work better when they are properly nourished? So, if we are going to go to the trouble of working out we may as well know what foods will optimize the results.

I was lucky enough to work with a top sports nutritionist to help his clients eat the right foods while they were training. I designed menu plans based around their dietary and training requirements, and even taught Premier League footballers how to cook! It was fascinating work and the most important thing I learnt was that if you lead an active life, or train as an athlete, there are specific foods to eat at specific times to help optimize your body's performance levels. The main rule is that to fuel your muscles before training you need some healthy, starchy carbohydrates, and after training you need to eat a small amount of healthy carbohydrates and proteins, as together they help to build muscle.

Muscles are predominantly made up of protein. We need to eat enough protein- and amino-acid-rich foods to replenish our muscle tissue and help it grow. Many animal products have all the amino acids we need to help our bodies build protein, foods like *lean meats*, including *chicken*, *turkey* and *beef*, *fish*, *cheese*, *eggs* and so on. You can also boost amino acids with plant-based sources of protein, but you will need to eat a wide variety to make sure you get them all. Good sources include *soy products* like *tofu*, *nuts*, *beans* and *pulses*, *lentils*, *legumes*, *whole grains* and *quinoa*.

A healthy supply of iron improves muscle performance. Iron helps produce red blood cells that carry oxygen to our muscles. The more oxygen our muscles have the longer they sustain physical activity. Good sources of iron include red meat, such as *steak* and *liver*, *oysters*, *chickpeas*, *soy beans*, *lentils* and *spinach*.

Vitamin C keeps blood vessels healthy. Blood vessels supply the muscles with all the nutrients you ingest and the oxygen produced as a result. A few good sources of vitamin C are *berries*, *citrus fruit*, *tomatoes* and *red (bell) peppers*.

Vitamin D helps with muscle movement. This vitamin is required for many functions within the muscles as they are being used, such as contraction, strength and growth. Good sources include *oily fish*, *mushrooms* (*Portobello*, *maitake*, *morel*), *tofu*, *soy yogurt*, *caviar*, *pork*, *eggs* and my favourite source of vitamin D: sunshine!

Calcium improves muscle tone and definition. In the body, calcium sends a signal to the muscles to contract. Without enough calcium, your muscles won't be able to perform properly and gain muscle tone. Calcium also keeps your bone structure and muscles strong. Great sources of calcium are *yogurt*, *sardines*, *spinach*, *white beans*, *figs*, *pak choi/bok choy*, *black strap molasses*, *kale*, *black-eyed beans*, *oranges*, *turnip greens*, *seaweed*, *tofu* and *soy milk*.

Fatty foods reduce inflammation and help muscles recover from strain or injury. Fats help keep the fluidity of the muscle's functions, reduce inflammation and help muscles to recover. It's a bit like keeping an engine well-oiled, we need to do the same with our muscles and joints. Muscles need good, unsaturated fats such as *fish oils*, *olive oil*, *peanut*, *walnut* and *flaxseed oils*. Plant-based sources include *avocados*, *algae oil* and *spirulina*.

Zinc encourages a quick metabolism. It assists the production of protein for muscle health and is found in high levels in *mushrooms*.

INGREDIENT	CONTENT	BEAUTY BENEFIT
Adzuki beans	Copper, folate, iron, magnesium, manganese, phosphorus, protein, selenium, sodium, vitamins B1 (thamin), B5 (pantothenic acid) and B6, zinc	Originating in Asia this small red bean is a powerhouse of protein, fibre and slow-releasing carbohydrates which are good for building muscle and providing energy. These beans also contain iron, vitamins and minerals, are low in fat and delicious.
Beef	Iron, phosphorus, potassium, protein, selenium, vitamins B3 (niacin), B6 and B12, zinc	Good-quality beef steak provides the body with all the essential amino acids needed for healthy growth and repair of all body tissue, including muscles. The iron levels also keep hair shiny and thick.
Black beans	Copper, fibre, folate, iron, manganese, magnesium, phosphorus, potassium, protein, vitamin B1 (thiamin)	Black beans contain plenty of healthy fibre for optimum digestion, are a good source of plant-based protein for keeping muscles strong and healthy, plus they contain a high level of anthocyanins which are known for their anti-aging properties.
Black strap molasses	Calcium, copper, iron, manganese, magnesium, potassium, selenium, vitamins B5 (pantothenic acid) and B6	Black strap molasses are a great source of iron, which is essential for healthy muscles. Iron deficiency leads to anaemia and hair loss. Lower in sugar than white refined sugar, molasses are a healthier option for adding sweetness to dishes and bakes.
Cherry tomatoes	Lycopene, potassium, vitamins A, C and K	Tomatoes contain vitamin C which aids the absorption of iron. They are also a great source of lycopene, which helps protect the skin from harmful UV rays and sun damage.
Chicken and turkey	Copper, iron, folate, omega-3, omega-6, phosphorous, protein, selenium, tryptophan, vitamins A, B2 (riboflavin), B3 (niacin), B5 (pantothenic acid), B6, B12 and C, zinc	Chicken and turkey are excellent sources of lean protein, which is used in every cell in our bodies to build and repair tissues, produce enzymes and hormones, and is the building block of bones, muscles, cartilage, skin and blood. Both also contain an amino acid called tryptophan, which increases the serotonin levels in your brain, relieving stress and enhancing your mood. And phosphorous builds strong bones and teeth.
Chickpeas	Choline, copper, fibre, folate, iron, magnesium, manganese, protein, phosphorus, vitamin B1 (thiamin)	Chickpeas, also known as 'garbanzo beans', are a complex carbohydrate from the legume family that are high in both protein and fibre. A plant-based protein and rich iron source they keep muscles strong.
Dark/bittersweet chocolate	Flavanols	The flavanols in chocolate are a type of flavonoid (antioxidant), which protects the skin from free radicals and sun damage, improves blood flow to the muscles, and reduces stress hormones.
Eggs	Folate, lutein, phosphorus, protein, selenium, vitamins A, B2 (riboflavin), B5 (pantothenic acid), B7 (biotin), B12 and D	Eggs as a whole are great for your hair, skin and nails. The lutein keeps skin elastic and hydrated, and the protein helps repair skin tissues and keeps hair strong and shiny. They also provide energy for exercise.
Ginger	Gingerol	The bioactive ingredient in ginger is called gingerol, which has powerful antioxidant and anti-inflammatory effects. It's widely known to ease the feeling of nausea and to help fight infection.
Nuts	Fibre, omega-3, omega-6, protein, vitamins B1 (thiamin), B2 (riboflavin), B3 (niacin), B6 , B12	Having a good variety of different nuts will provide your muscles with all the essential fatty acids they need to reduce any swelling or inflammation in tired limbs, and also keep skin plump and young.
Quinoa	Copper, fibre, folate, iron, protein, lysine, magnesium, phosphorus, vitamins B1 (thiamin) and B2 (riboflavin)	Quinoa is an excellent source of plant-based protein that contains all nine essential amino acids. It's also a great source of iron and fibre. Iron is needed in the production of red blood cells which carry oxygen to all our cells, and is vital to keeping hair and muscles strong and healthy.
Tahini	Copper, iron, phosphorus, protein, manganese, omega-3, omega-6, vitamin B1 (thiamin)	Made from ground sesame seeds, tahini contains high levels of B-vitamins and iron, which play an important role in keeping our red blood cells healthy so they can transport enough oxygen to our muscles. Tahini's omega-3 fatty acids also helps detoxify the liver.

DIGESTION

The recipes in this book that promote good digestion are designed to keep your gut healthy and running smoothly. The digestive system plays an outstandingly huge role in your beauty regime and is not to be neglected just because we can't see it. The digestive system is the place where all the good nutrients needed to feed our skin, hair, nails and so on, are absorbed into the blood stream, and where toxins are eliminated.

If our digestive system isn't working properly or isn't able to eliminate toxins effectively it will use other organs to help do its job. Seeing as our skin is our biggest organ, bad digestion can cause a whole host of problems such as breakouts, acne, dermatitis, eczema and dull skin. Having bad digestion can be caused by a number of things including stress, eating foods that your body is sensitive to, not enough exercise, eating highly processed or sugary foods and being dehydrated.

Key points to remember for keeping your gut healthy are to drink plenty of water, eat fibrous foods and probiotics, plus cut out processed sugary foods altogether!

Water is key to good digestion. Staying hydrated helps the body eliminate all the toxins within it and makes it easier for stools to pass. Not having enough water in your system slows the process down, causes constipation and also restricts the stomach in being able to produce enough of the right acids to digest food properly. A good check to know if you're drinking enough water is to make sure your pee is clear all day. Always carry a bottle of water with you when you're on the move.

Fibre is essential to regular flushing of toxins. Along with drinking enough water, we also need a good amount of fibre to help keep us regular and things moving. Fibre bulks up our stools, making sure the waste keeps moving. It also helps regulate how quickly glucose is entered into the blood stream, keeping blood sugar levels even. Some fibre, called 'prebiotics', helps boost the good bacteria that transform into probiotics in the digestive tract. The probiotics feed off the prebiotics. Top prebiotic foods are *bananas, whole wheat* and *corn*. Here are some great sources of fibrous foods you should make sure you stock up on: *lentils, black beans, lima beans, artichokes, peas, broccoli, Brussels sprouts, raspberries, blackberries, avocados, pears, bran flakes, whole wheat pasta, chia seeds, flaxseeds/linseeds, oatmeal, porridge oats, chickpeas* and *farro*.

Probiotics are essential for a healthy gut. These are the good live bacteria that live in our gut and help aid digestion in several ways by eliminating toxins, aiding the absorption of vitamins and minerals and the optimal digestion of foods. There are some 'bad' bacterias that also live in our gut and it's important to make sure the balance is right. Eating too many processed and sugary foods can feed the bad bacteria, causing an overgrowth, which can lead to health problems such as candida, depression and a poor or weakened immune system. Good sources of natural probiotics include *tempeh, kimchi, natural live yogurt, pickles, microalgae,* such as *spirulina, chlorella* and *blue green algae, ginger, kombucha, sauerkraut, kefir* and *miso soup.*

Fatty acids help to heal inflammation in the gut. Often prescribed for conditions such as Irritable Bowel Syndrome (IBS), good sources of ingredients that contain fatty acids like DHA, omega-3 and omega-6 include *algae oil, spelt* and *spirulina.*

B-vitamins flush out toxins and support kidney function. Good plant sources include antioxidant-rich *papaya* and *parsley.*

INGREDIENT	CONTENT	BEAUTY BENEFIT
Amaranth	Fibre, folate, iron, magnesium, manganese, phosphorus, protein, selenium, vitamin B6	A gluten-free grain that is high in protein and dietary fibre, is easily digestible and helps prevent constipation. As a good source of iron it can encourage red blood cell production, which can ensure movement of oxygen.
Apple cider vinegar	Acetic, citric and malic acids, manganese, protein, probiotic bacteria	Apple cider vinegar is antibacterial, anti-fungal, anti-viral and anti-inflammatory. Known to help maintain beautiful skin by restoring and balancing the skins pH levels, essential to preventing breakouts.
Apples	Fibre, vitamin C	Vitamin C is essential for collagen production in the skin and also keeps us regular with the easily digestible fibre in apples. There's a lot of goodness in the apple skin so try to eat that, too.
Apricots	Fibre, iron, potassium, vitamins A and C	Apricots are a great source of iron and dietary fibre. They aid digestion and can treat constipation. Apricot oil is good for the skin and has healthy amounts of vitamin A and antioxidants that protect the skin from damage.
Artichokes	Copper, fibre, folate, magnesium, manganese, phosphorus, potassium, vitamins C and K	Artichokes contain a rich supply of antioxidants which keep the skin smooth and wrinkle-free, plus they help detoxify the liver and digestive system. The high levels of dietary fibre help keep bowel movements regular and help our bodies eliminate toxins for clearer looking skin.
Banana	Fibre, folate, magnesium, manganese, potassium, vitamins B6, B7 (biotin) and C	A source of fibre to aid digestion, plus a great natural source of energy. Bananas are rich in potassium and moisture, which is hydrating for dry skin, while the lectin in bananas destroys the bacteria that causes acne.
Baobab fruit powder	Calcium, magnesium, manganese, potassium, vitamins B1 (thiamin) and C	The baobab fruit is a nutrient superfood from Africa. It supports healthy digestion, immunity and nourishes skin. High levels of vitamin C help the skin form collagen and elastin, which support the skin's structure, keeping it wrinkle free. Antioxidants fight skin-damaging free radicals.
Black rice	Anthocyanins, copper, fibre, iron, magnesium, manganese, phosphorus, protein, zinc	Black rice is a great source of fibre, which aids digestion by binding to toxins and helping push them out of the body. The high level of antioxidants in black rice detoxes the body and aids liver function.
Chia seeds	Calcium, fibre, manganese, omega-3, omega-6, phosphorus, protein	Omega-3 fats help treat acne, smooth wrinkles, and keep hair and nails strong and shiny. Chia seeds are also a great source of fibre, protein and vitamin E for other bodily functions.
Cumin	Iron, manganese, vitamin B1 (thiamin)	The iron levels in cumin seeds make them good for energy and making red blood cells. They also stimulate the pancreatic enzymes needed for proper digestion.
Daikon radish	Calcium, copper, fibre, folate, magnesium, potassium, vitamin C	Health benefits include immunity, reduced inflammation, good digestion, detoxifying weight loss and bone health. It is also a natural diuretic.
Fermented vegetables	Probiotic bacteria	Fermented vegetables, such as kimchi, contain probiotics (friendly bacteria) that aid digestive health, balance the production of stomach acids and help increase bowel movement.
Flaxseeds/linseeds	Calcium, copper, fibre, folate, iron, lignans, magnesium, manganese, omega-3, potassium, protein, selenium, vitamins B1 (thiamin), B2 (riboflavin), B3 (niacin), B5 (pantothetic acid), B6 and K, zinc	Flaxseeds/linseeds are rich in omega-3 fatty acids, which help the growth of new skin cells, keep skin hydrated and wrinkles at bay, while keeping hair strong, too. Regular consumption of flaxseeds/linseeds can help with skin conditions such as acne, eczema, psoriasis and dermatitis. They also have such a good levels of insoluble and soluble fibre that they really help the intestinal tract push out waste and at the same time absorb the nutrients the body needs.
Garlic	Allicin, calcium, copper, fibre, iron, manganese, phosphorus, protein, potassium, sulphur, selenium, vitamins B1 (thiamin), B6, C, zinc	Garlic has been used for its antibacterial and medicinal properties for centuries. It acts as a blood thinner enabling blood flow and contains high levels of allicin, which is anti-fungal and is said to have skin-soothing and anti-aging benefits. But take note, too much can irritate the gut.

INGREDIENT	CONTENT	BEAUTY BENEFIT
Ghee	Butyric acid, vitamins A, D, E and K2	Ghee is a clarified butter originating from India. It's a great source of omega-3 fatty acids, which revitalize and hydrate skin from the inside out. Rich in antioxidants that help protect the skin from free radical damage, it's also known to help detoxify the body and supply energy. The butyric acid keeps the intestinal wall healthy, which in turn aids digestion.
Grapes	Anthocyanins, manganese, vitamin K	Black grapes are said to be the healthiest of all, due to the high levels of anthocyanins, which give the black pigmentation. They are powerful antioxidants that help protect our skin from free-radical damage.
Green/French beans	Calcium, copper, fibre, folate, iron, magnesium, manganese, phosphorus, potassium, protein, vitamins A, B1 (thiamin), B2 (riboflavin), B3 (niacin), B5 (pantothetic acid), B6 and C, zinc	Green/French beans are low in calories and a good source of vitamin A and C. Our bodies uses vitamin A and C to help keep our immune systems strong, and also for healthy skin and eye functions.
Inca/golden berries	Bioflavanoids, phytochemicals, vitamins A, B12 and C	Inca/golden berries are an Ancient, nutritious superfood, with high levels of antioxidants and anti-inflammatory bioflavonoids. High in fibre, they are great for digestive health.
Kefir	Probiotic bacteria, protein	Kefir is a potent probiotic, making it excellent for digestive health. The friendly bacteria help balance gut health ensuring that our food gets digested correctly. Kefir is also a great source of calcium for keeping bones strong and healthy.
Mint	Vitamin A	The strong aroma of mint alone is used to clear blocked noses and acts as a stimulant to awaken the senses. The smell activates your salivary glands, which produce enzymes to help you digest food better. It also soothes indigestion.
Miso paste	Calcium, copper, fibre, folate, iron, magnesium, manganese, omega-3 and 6, probiotic bacteria, protein, selenium, sodium, vitamins B2 (riboflavin), B6 and K, zinc	Miso paste has many health benefits including, anti-aging, improving mood, reducing stress and anxiety, bone health, strong immune system and improved digestion. Miso paste is made from fermented soy beans that provide friendly bacteria called probiotics that keep the gut in balance.
Oats	Calcium, iron, fibre, folate, magnesium, manganese, phosphorus, selenium, vitamins A, B1 (thiamin), B2 (riboflavin), B3 (niacin), B6,	Oats are full of dietary fibre, which aids digestion, the absorption of nutrients, keeps blood-sugar levels balanced and helps with eliminating toxins. They are also a slow-releasing carbohydrate, making them ideal for breakfast dishes or snacks before a session at the gym.
Peanuts	Calcium, copper, fibre, folate, iron, magnesium, manganese, mono-unsaturated fat, phosphorus, potassium, protein, resveratrol, vitamins B1 (thiamin), B2 (riboflavin), B3 (niacin), B6, zinc	Peanuts are a great natural source of energy and their monounsaturated fats and antioxidants help keep your heart healthy. Peanuts also contain resveratrol which is a potent anti aging phytochemical.
Popcorn	Insoluble fibre	Popcorn is full of insoluble fibre, which sweeps through the digestive tract and taking food particles along with any toxins and eliminating them. Too many toxins in the body can come out as pimples on the skin.
Pears	Fibre, magnesium, vitamin C	Pears are a great source of dietary fibre, which keeps our digestive systems healthy and is able to flush out toxins. It also slows the release of sugars into our blood stream, which can damage collagen production.
Tarragon	Phytonutrients	Tarragon is most commonly known to relieve digestive problems because it encourages production of bile by the liver. Bile is produced to absorb fats and eliminate waste.

BONES AND TEETH

When I wrote this book I didn't want it to be just about external beauty (the bits people can see). I want this book to have a whole body beauty regime, inside and out. I felt it imperative to highlight the importance of keeping our bones and teeth healthy. To have a beautiful smile we need healthy teeth and gums; to have a beautiful posture we need strong bones. As children, our bones are constantly growing, until we reach our twenties when it begins to really slow down, and then we hit our thirties and pretty much all bone growth deposits are done. Bone density slowly begins to diminish as we get older. The chronic condition of this is called osteoporosis, which makes your bones very weak, brittle and prone to fractures. The good news is that we can do a few things to help protect our bones and keep them strong. The easiest way is by eating a diet full of foods that contain the nutrients your bones and teeth need. You must also keep active. Bones are living structures that are constantly working to rebuild and repair. They are made up of protein, connective tissues, blood vessels and nerves, and our bodies build a new skeleton every ten years.

Calcium and vitamin D are essential for bone growth. The two work together as vitamin D helps the body absorb the calcium for bone growth, and calcium helps support teeth and bone structure. Good sources of calcium are *yogurt, cheese, milk, Chinese cabbage, sardines, white beans, figs, pak choi/bok choy, black strap molasses, kale, black-eyed beans, oranges, turnip and beetroot/beet greens, seaweed, tofu and soy milk*. Great sources of vitamin D are *oily fish, mushrooms, tofu, soy yogurt, caviar, pork, eggs* and some sunshine – but please don't forget the sun protection!

Vitamin K2 navigates calcium straight to bones and teeth. K2 is a very interesting vitamin when looking at bone nutrition. It helps guide the calcium to where it needs to go. Good sources are *dairy products, red meat* and *poultry*. If you're vegan, a good source is a Japanese food called 'natto' which is a form of fermented soy bean.

All minerals and vitamins are good for strong bones. But some of the most important minerals and vitamins that we should make sure we have enough of are phosphorus, magnesium, B-vitamins, vitamin E and adequate protein from nutritional powerhouses, like *seaweed* and *spinach*.

There are foods to avoid. We need also to be mindful of consuming caffeinated and sugary foods, as they have negative effects on bone health as well as many other detrimental health affects. Too much coffee, salt, alcohol and certain medications should be avoided.

INGREDIENT	CONTENT	BEAUTY BENEFIT
Coriander/cilantro	Essential oils, vitamins A and K	Coriander/cilantro has the highest amount of vitamin K of all herbs. Vitamin K plays a role in building bone mass. It also has muscle-relaxing qualities, calming the nerves, which helps us get a better beauty sleep.
Farro	B-vitamins, fibre, iron, protein, magnesium, zinc	Farro is an excellent source of fibre, plant-based proteins, iron, zinc, magnesium and B-vitamins. This grain is a good source of antioxidants called lignans, which reduce inflammation and keep the heart healthy.
Feta	Calcium, omega-3, omega-6, protein, phosphorus, selenium, sodium, vitamins A, B1 (thiamin), B2 (riboflavin), B5 (pantothenic acid), B6, B12, zinc	Feta is lower in fat and calories than most cheeses. A good source of protein for people who don't eat meat. Calcium is an essential mineral for healthy and strong bones and teeth.
Figs	Calcium, fibre, magnesium, manganese, vitamins B6 and K	Figs are an all-round nutritious superfruit. They are high in calcium, which is the most important mineral for building bones. They also contain phosphorus which encourages regrowth after damage caused by injury.
Mackerel	DHA fatty acids, omega-3, magnesium, phosphorus, potassium, protein, selenium, vitamins B1 (thiamin), B2 (riboflavin), B3 (niacin), B5 (pantothenic acid), B6, B12, D	Mackerel is an excellent source of essential fatty acids and omega-3s. These are needed for brain function, healthy hearts, blood circulation, healthy cholesterol levels and much more. For bone health, it contains a good amount of calcium which is needed to keep bones strong, and is anti-inflammatory so helps to relieve joint pain for people who suffer from arthritis.
Milk (dairy and nut)	Calcium, phosphorus, protein, selenium, vitamins A, B2 (riboflavin), B7 (biotin), B12, D and E	Milk is a good source of calcium and phosphorus, both of which are needed to keep bones and teeth strong and healthy. Most dairy milk is fortified with vitamin D, which helps the calcium to be absorbed better. Vegan nut milks contain a good amount of dairy and vitamin D.
Mushrooms (especially shiitake)	Calcium, copper, vitamins B2 (riboflavin), B3 (niacin), B12 and D	Mushrooms contain anti-inflammatory enzymes, which ease skin conditions such as rosacea, eczema and acne. They also provide an excellent source of copper that keeps blood, bones, joints and skin healthy.
Parsley	Copper, folate, iron, vitamins A, C, and K, zinc	Parsley is packed full of vitamins and minerals and can detoxify the body by flushing out excess liquids and supporting kidney function.
Pineapple	Folic acid, manganese, vitamins B1 (thiamin), B6 and C	Pineapples are anti-inflammatory and rich in manganese, which is vital for bone growth, strengthening and improving connective tissues.
Sardines	Calcium, iron, magnesium, omega-3, omega-6, phosphorus, potassium, protein, selenium, vitamins B2 (riboflavin), B3 (niacin), B5 (pantothenic acid), B6, B12, D, E	Sardines can help keep skin, bones and teeth healthy as they contain high amounts of omega-3 fatty acids, calcium, phosphorus and vitamin D. These nutrients can help prevent bone mineral loss and speed up the healing caused by bone injury.
Soy products	Copper, selenium, zinc	It's best to buy non-GMO branded soy products. They are great plant-based sources of proteins, amino acids and calcium for bones and teeth.
Spelt	Amino acids, fibre, iron, magnesium, manganese, protein, phosphorus, selenium, vitamins B1 (thiamin) and B3 (niacin), zinc	Spelt is one of the oldest crops recorded in history. Its health benefits include regulating metabolism, increasing circulation, building strong bones, improving digestion and lowering blood sugar levels.
Spirulina	Amino acids, protein, phytonutrients	This blue-green algae is a must for strengthening bones, helping with anaemia, giving glowing skin and strong shiny hair.
Tofu	Amino acids, beta-carotene, calcium, copper, fibre, GLA fatty acids, omega-6, phosphorus, phytonutrients, protein, manganese, selenium, vitamins B1 (thiamin), D	Tofu is a low-carbohydrate, low-cholesterol, plant-based source of protein, calcium and vitamin D, which are essential for muscle and bone health. Vitamin D helps the body absorb the calcium more easily. Tofu also helps build skin elasticity and keratin for shiny strong hair.

I thought it quite crucial to have a chapter in this book just for drinks. Having a juice or smoothie every day is a brilliant way to pack a bunch of essential beauty nutrients into your daily diet. It's quick, easy and you can drink it on the way to work, when dropping the kids off or heading to the gym. These are some of my favourite drink recipes for keeping every part of you beautiful, and don't forget to keep yourself hydrated and drink plenty of water, too!

Drinks

Many people find that just eating avocados regularly can do wonders for your skin. I try to have a quarter or half every day. Avocados are packed full of oleic acid, an omega-9 fatty acid, and healthy monounsaturated fats. These play a very important role as one of the building blocks of healthy skin by keeping the epidermal layer of the skin soft and hydrated. Oleic acid also helps regenerate damaged skin cells and reduces facial redness. Avocados are also an excellent source of vitamin E, antioxidant carotenoids and vitamin C.

S H AVOCADO SMOOTHIE

1 ripe avocado, peeled and stoned/pitted
240 ml/1 scant cup almond milk or milk of your choosing
2 tablespoons honey

1½ cups ice cubes
a tiny pinch of salt

a high-speed blender

SERVES 2

Add all the ingredients to a blender and whizz until you have a really smooth smoothie. You can add more milk if you prefer it to be a little runnier, and if you prefer it sweeter just add a little more honey.

NOTE High in unsaturated fats, this is great for complexion and hair strength.

BLUEBERRY, BLACKBERRY AND MORINGA SMOOTHIE

Blueberries and blackberries are great for your skin as they contain high amounts of vitamin C amongst many other vitamins and nutrients. Vitamin C is essential for the development and maintenance of scar tissue, blood vessels and cartilage, which in turn helps reduce fine lines and wrinkles. Plus these berries have high levels of antioxidants to help protect skin, too. Moringa is a superfood sold in powder form. First discovered in India, the moringa tree now grows in many tropical and sub-tropical countries. Best known for its high level of vitamin C (seven times more than an orange) and iron (25 times more than spinach), it has high levels of vitamin A and several B-vitamins, plus protein and calcium.

250 g/2 cups fresh or
frozen blueberries
130 g/1 cup fresh
blackberries
2 teaspoons moringa
powder

1 banana
750 ml/3 cups apple
juice

a high-speed blender

SERVES 2

Add all the ingredients to a blender and whizz to a smooth liquid. Pour and serve.

(S) (M) LINGONBERRY AND STRAWBERRY SMOOTHIE

Lingonberries, from Scandinavia, are in the cranberry, bilberry and blueberry family. They have high concentrations of plant polyphenols and numerous health benefits. One of the most important benefits with regards to keeping your skin healthy, is that lingonberries are reported to help the body replace important antioxidants, which help to nourish and protect our blood vessels and tissue cells.

125 g/1 cup fresh or frozen lingonberries
100 g/1 cup fresh strawberries, hulled
½ banana
500 ml/2 cups orange juice
1–2 tablespoons honey

a high-speed blender

SERVES 2

Add all the ingredients to a blender and whizz to a smooth liquid. Pour and serve.

(H) (S) (D) BAOBAB LEMONADE

This is my ultimate lazy recipe which is also incredibly good for you. The sweet and tangy baobab fruit is a nutrient powerhouse and superfood. Its high dosage of vitamin C helps the skin to form collagen and elastin, plus its incredible antioxidant properties help nourish the skin, boost your immune system and provide plenty of natural energy.

1 lemon, quartered, plus slices of lemon to serve
140 g/½ cup honey
750 ml/3 cups filtered water
3 tablespoons baobab fruit powder
ice cubes, to serve

a high-speed blender

SERVES 4

Pop the lemon quarters into a blender. Add the honey and half of the water and whizz until everything has been blitzed.

Pour the liquid through a fine-mesh sieve or strainer into a jug/pitcher and discard all the bits. Pour the liquid back into the blender. Add the rest of the water and the baobab fruit powder and give it another whizz to blend everything together.

Taste to see if it's sweet enough for you – you can always add more honey if you want. I like mine a little bitter and tangy.

Serve with ice and a slice!

H D COCONUT AND GHEE COFFEE

I do quite like my coffee in the morning and one way to make it even more beneficial, apart from waking me up, is to add a spoonful of ghee (clarified butter). It turns the coffee creamy and frothy which is just how I like it.

250 ml/1 cup freshly brewed organic coffee

2 teaspoons organic grass-fed ghee

2 tablespoons light coconut milk

1 teaspoon honey (optional)

a high-speed blender

SERVES 2

Add all the ingredients to a blender and blend for about 30 seconds on high until lovely and frothy. Pour and drink straight away.

H S STRAWBERRY, RASPBERRY AND ALMOND MILK SMOOTHIE

This smoothie is full of the lustrous hair-boosting vitamin biotin which plays a very important role in keeping your locks strong and luscious. Found in almond milk, strawberries and raspberries, this smoothie will do wonders for your hair.

100 g/½ cup frozen strawberries

100 g/½ cup frozen raspberries, plus extra to garnish

60 g/½ cup sliced frozen banana

250 ml/1 cup almond milk

1 tablespoon honey or agave syrup

TO GARNISH
1 fresh strawberry, sliced
3–4 fresh raspberries

a high-speed blender

SERVES 1

Simply blend all the ingredients in a blender until no lumps are left. Pour, top with a few extra raspberries and serve.

TIP I like to freeze my berries so that when I make the smoothies I don't have to add any ice. You can use the berries un-frozen and fresh also.

Ghee

Ghee has been used in anti-aging beauty rituals and keeping hair strong and healthy for centuries in India. Thinking about it, all my Indian friends have thick, long, luscious hair to die for – perhaps eating and drinking ghee is their secret! It's said a little every day provides you with plenty of healthy essential fats and it is also rich in vitamins A, D, K2 and E and antioxidants.

E SPINACH, KALE AND CARROT JUICE

Raw carrot juice is an excellent source of beta-carotene which is converted to vitamin A in our bodies and is essential to helping the eye retina function properly. The spinach and kale are a great source of carotenoids which are an antioxidant that helps promote healthy eyes and prevents macular degeneration. Freshly pressed juice is such a great way to start the day and get all your vitamins and minerals.

50 g/1 cup spinach
  leaves
30 g/1 cup kale
1 apple, cored
3 carrots, trimmed

a 2.5-cm/1-inch piece
  of fresh ginger

a cold-press juicer

SERVES 1

Pop all the ingredients in a juicer and juice away until smooth. Pour and serve immediately.

S D POMEGRANATE, STRAWBERRY AND CHIA JUICE

Pomegranates are full of ellagic acid which helps promote collagen production in the skin. Plus they're packed full of vitamin C and antioxidants. Combined with the chia seeds (full of omega-3s and omega-6s), this is a drink your skin will love you for, and it's super refreshing!

1 tablespoon chia seeds
200 g/1 cup frozen
  strawberries
250 ml/1 cup
  pomegranate juice

a high-speed blender

SERVES 1

Soak the chia seeds in 200 ml/¾ cup of water for 30 minutes. Blend the strawberries and pomegranate juice together in a blender, pour in the soaked chia seeds (with any water that may not be absorbed) and give it one more blend together. Pour and serve for a refreshingly tasty skin-boosting tonic.

CHOCOLATE FLAXSEED SMOOTHIE

D S

This smoothie has a good dose of ground flaxseeds/linseeds, which are a great source of soluble fibre that helps the elimination process. Flaxseeds/linseeds are also packed full of lignans and omega-3 fats. Lignans are an antioxidant phytonutrient that reduces cholesterol and the risk of cardiovascular disease. Omega-3s are a natural anti-inflammatory so can help with any inflammation problems in the digestive tract.

1½ tablespoons pure cocoa powder
1 tablespoon dark/bittersweet chocolate chips
1 frozen peeled banana
250 ml/1 cup almond milk
2 tablespoons ground flaxseeds/linseeds
1 tablespoon agave syrup dark/bittersweet chocolate shavings, to garnish

a high-speed blender

SERVES 1

Simply pop all the ingredients into a blender and blend until smooth. Pour, garnish with chocolate shavings and serve.

NOTE Depending on the capacity of your blender you could double, triple or quadruple the ingredients here to make a larger batch of smoothies to share.

ULTIMATE MUSCLE SMOOTHIE

M

This smoothie is designed to have everything your muscles need to stay strong and working like a well looked after machine. The vitamin C from the berries and orange juice helps to keep your blood vessels strong, pumping oxygen and nutrients all around your body to all of the muscles. The spinach and dried figs are a good plant source of calcium which is needed for your muscles to perform properly and keep your bone structure strong. The soy yogurt is a good source of vitamin D and plant protein which help aid muscle growth, contraction and strength.

150 g/1 cup mixed frozen berries
170 g/1 small pot vanilla soy yogurt
50 g/1 cup baby spinach leaves
2 dried figs, stalks cut off
250 ml/1 cup fresh orange juice
1 tablespoon protein powder (optional)

TO GARNISH (OPTIONAL)
dark/bittersweet chocolate shavings
orange peel

a high-speed blender

SERVES 1

Simply blend all the ingredients together in a blender until smooth. Pour, garnish with chocolate shavings and a twist of orange peel, if desired, and serve for an excellent dose of everything your muscles need to stay strong, firm and healthy.

FLAVOURED WATER

A key beauty tip my mother always reinforced was to keep hydrated and drink plenty of water. So simple yet absolutely essential to keep your skin looking youthful. Our bodies are made of 55–75 per cent water so we need to be mindful to replenish ourselves at regular intervals. When our skin is fully hydrated fine lines are less visible as they are filled in when plump. Water helps carry all the essential nutrients and oxygen to our cells, as well as flush toxins out. It helps to prevent constipation and keep our digestion in top form, regulate body temperature, keep our joints lubricated as well as many other key functions. Here are a few ingredients you can add to your water to add a hint of flavour and keep it interesting.

ice cubes
1 litre/4 cups purified
    water

CALMING CUCUMBER
5 fresh mint leaves
5 cucumber slices
2 lime slices

CITRUS BURST
2 orange slices
2 lemon slices
2 lime slices

VERY BERRY
1 strawberry, sliced
5 raspberries
5 blackberries
2 tablespoons chia seeds

IMMUNE BOOSTER
2 lemon slices
3 fresh ginger slices
2 lemongrass stalks,
    outer leaf discarded
    and sliced in half
    lengthways
5 fresh mint leaves

REFRESHER
200 g/1 cup watermelon
    chunks
3 lime slices

EACH SERVES 4

For each flavoured water, put the ingredients into a jug/pitcher and gently squish or muddle the fruit to release the flavours. Add some ice and pour the water over. Give it a stir and leave to sit for at least 30 minutes.

Strain the water into glasses to stop all the bits going in and serve.

NOTE Water is best served at tepid temperature for digestion but you can store the flavoured waters in the fridge for a day or two.

Water

Water is vital for life, for all bodily functions and is an essential nutrient. Every cell in our bodies needs water to work properly. In relation to beauty, water helps flush out toxins keeping skin clear and pores clean. It also hydrates all the cells in the skin's surface, keeping skin looking firm and tight and reducing the appearance of wrinkles. Drinking enough water makes your blood thinner and thus more efficient in carrying nutrients around the body and reaching cells quicker.

S B CALCIUM CHAI
H E GREEN SMOOTHIE

For those who choose not to (or cannot) have dairy in their diet it's important to remember to include enough calcium from alternative sources. All the ingredients in this smoothie are packed full of calcium from plant sources, with a touch of chai spice, making this a delicious way to keep your bones and teeth strong and healthy.

½ tablespoon dried seaweed

50 g/1 cup baby spinach leaves

30 g/1 cup baby kale

250 ml/1 cup soy or almond milk

3 dried figs, stalks removed

2 teaspoons chai tea powder (or 125 ml/ ½ cup chai tea concentrate)

a high-speed blender

SERVES 1

Soak the dried seaweed in 250 ml/1 cup of water for 15 minutes to rehydrate it. Once it is soft, add it to a blender with all the other ingredients, discarding the water, and blend until smooth. Pour the creamy green goodness into glasses and enjoy.

TIP Be sure to rinse the baby spinach and kale to get rid of any grit before blending.

NOTE Depending on the capacity of your blender you could double, triple or quadruple the ingredients here to make a larger batch of smoothies to share.

Baby spinach, baby kale and other leafy greens

Spinach is high in calcium, rich in antioxidants and vitamins, and also contains high levels of iron and essential minerals to keep blood cells healthy and carrying oxygen to all our muscles. Kale has so many great beauty benefits for our skin, hair and nails as it's packed with antioxidants and essential vitamins and minerals. For bone health, both are great plant-based sources of calcium and also contain vitamin K which helps the body know where to use the calcium.

What better way to start your day than by having a breakfast packed full of beautiful nutrients that you know your body will love and thank you for. I'm a big fan of brunch, so some of the recipes are designed for a more leisurely and slow-paced day where you have more time to whip up some eggs or do a bit of baking. The other recipes are for my usual pace, which is fast and on-the-go, and just require throwing everything into a bowl.

Breakfasts

D S SUPER BERRY GRANOLA

Super berries, such as açai, goji, inca/golden, cranberries and blueberries, to name a few, have been hailed as anti-aging superfoods due to their high levels of antioxidants, vitamins and phytochemicals that help to keep your skin glowing. Nowadays you can buy mixed bags of these super berries and I like to add them to my homemade, gluten-free granola every morning.

300 g/3 cups gluten-free or steel-cut oats
70 g/½ cup flaked/slivered almonds
75 g/1 cup desiccated/shredded coconut
80 g/½ cup chia seeds
70 g/½ cup pumpkin seeds
70 g/½ cup sunflower seeds
a pinch of salt

125 g/scant ½ cup honey, plus extra to serve
125 ml/½ cup algae, coconut or sunflower oil
150 g/1 cup mixed dried super berries
plain yogurt, to serve

SERVES 8–10

Preheat the oven to 150°C (300°F) Gas 2.

Put the oats, almonds, coconut, chia, pumpkin and sunflower seeds, plus a pinch of salt in a large mixing bowl and give it a good stir together. Drizzle the honey and oil over the top and stir in. Once the mixture starts clumping together and everything is coated in honey and oil, spread it out onto a couple of baking sheets and pop into the preheated oven to cook for 30 minutes. Give the granola a couple of stirs while it's cooking to make sure everything is evenly baked. It will be a lovely golden colour and crisp texture when cooked.

Remove from the oven and leave to cool.

Once cooled, stir in the super berries and keep in an airtight container for up to 2 weeks. Serve with yogurt and a drizzle of extra honey if desired.

D S BANANA, CHOCOLATE AND CHIA NO-COOK OATS

Oats are full of soluble fibre which helps aid digestion. Unprocessed steel-cut oats are also a slow-digesting carbohydrate, which means they keep you fuller for longer. This easy breakfast should keep tummies full until lunchtime. The tiny but powerful chia seeds absorb water and become gel-like, expanding in the stomach. This helps give a feeling of fullness. Chia seeds are also an excellent source of fibre, some say one of the best in the world. And lastly, the cocoa and banana will give you a boost of energy as well as tasting delicious.

½ banana, mashed
70 g/½ cup steel-cut oats
250 ml/1 cup almond milk
2 teaspoons pure cocoa powder
1 tablespoon honey
2 teaspoons chia seeds

a 300–500-ml/ 10–17-fl. oz. capacity sterilized glass jar with an airtight lid

SERVES 1

Mix all the ingredients together in the glass jar. Cover and shake together.

Leave in the fridge overnight. In the morning your breakfast will be ready! Take out and eat straight away or take to work or school with you.

D S PEAR, APPLE AND BLACKBERRY COMPOTE

I like to have this compote on top of my Super Berry Granola (page 42) or porridge to brighten it up and add an extra dose of vitamins and minerals. Pears help keep you regular as they are packed full of fibre which is essential for a healthy digestive system.

2 pears (I use Comice pears), cored and diced
2 apples, peeled, cored and diced
50 g/¼ cup raw demerara/turbinado sugar
¼ teaspoon ground cinnamon
300 g/2¼ cups blackberries

SERVES 8

Put the diced pears and apples into a saucepan with 2 tablespoons of water, the sugar and cinnamon. Set over medium heat and simmer gently for 10 minutes, then add the blackberries and continue to simmer gently for a further 10 minutes until the juices are thick.

Take off the heat and cool before serving.

Apples and pears

Eating an apple or pear a day can make skin glow and encourage regular bowel movement with easily digestible fibre. Dietary fibre keeps the digestive system healthy and able to flush out toxins, keeping skin clear. Fibre also helps slow the release of sugars into our blood stream. A sudden spike in sugar can damage collagen on the skin's surface. There's a lot of fibrous goodness in the skins of apples and pears, so leave the skin on as much as possible.

ⓈHEMP BREAD

Hemp seeds contain over 30 per cent fat – the good fats which our skin needs to stay firm. The two richest fatty acids contained in the seeds are omega-6 and omega-3. They are also a great source of vitamin E and other minerals.

1 x 7-g/¼-oz. packet fast-action dried yeast
2 tablespoons honey
250 ml/1 cup warm water
400 g/3 cups spelt flour
1 teaspoon salt
30 g/½ cup hemp seeds, plus extra to sprinkle
1 tablespoon olive oil
1 beaten egg (optional)

TO SERVE
Peanut Butter (see right)
clementine segments

a 900-g/2-lb. loaf pan, dusted with spelt flour

MAKES 1 LOAF AND SERVES 4–6

Mix the yeast, honey and warm water together in a small mixing bowl. Leave somewhere warm for 10 minutes to activate the yeast – the mixture will become frothy.

Put the spelt flour, salt and hemp seeds into a separate large mixing bowl and stir together. Make a well in the middle of the bowl. When the yeast mixture is ready, pour it into the centre, add the oil and stir everything together until it starts to come together as a dough. Use your hands to form a ball.

Tip the dough onto a lightly floured work surface and knead it for 8 minutes, until smooth and stretchy. Return the dough to the bowl, cover with a damp kitchen cloth and leave in a warm place for 1½ hours, or until doubled in size.

Knock out the air from the dough and tip out onto a floured work surface to give it another quick knead (just for a couple of minutes this time). Put the dough into the loaf pan, cover again with a damp kitchen cloth and leave somewhere warm for 30 minutes. It will settle in the pan and rise again.

Preheat the oven to 200°C (400°F) Gas 6.

I like to brush the top of my loaf with beaten egg so that I get a hard crust. This is optional. Sprinkle about 1 tablespoon of extra hemp seeds on top to garnish the loaf.

Pop into the preheated oven to bake for 25–30 minutes. A good way to test if it is cooked through is when you take the loaf out of the oven, it will be firm and the top should be hard when tapped. Take the loaf out of the pan and turn it upside down, knock the bottom of the loaf and it should sound hollow when properly baked all the way through.

Leave to cool, then serve – I love to spread slices of this bread with a thick layer of peanut butter and serve segments of fresh clementines on the side.

ⒹPEANUT BUTTER

125 g/1 cup roasted and lightly salted peanuts
1 tablespoon raw brown sugar or coconut sugar
1 tablespoon peanut oil

a food processor

MAKES 125 ML/½ CUP

Add all the ingredients to a food processor and blend until smooth. Done.

NOTE The peanut butter can be kept in an airtight container for up to a month in the fridge. You can use unsalted peanuts if you prefer, or add less or more sugar depending on taste. You can even use different nuts; almonds or cashews are delicious. Enjoy experimenting with what suits you.

GLUTEN-FREE BREAKFAST TACOS WITH EGG, SWISS CHARD AND MUSHROOMS

Hair is made from a form of protein called keratin. Biotin is needed to help the body break down proteins and produce keratin, and it has rejuvenating properties that help cell regeneration. Eggs and Swiss chard are great sources of natural biotin, and the mushrooms are packed full of vitamin D – also essential for a healthy head of hair.

4 eggs
3 tablespoons whole, soy or almond milk
1½ tablespoons extra virgin olive oil
½ small red onion, thinly sliced
½ teaspoon fresh or dried thyme leaves, plus extra to garnish
65 g/1 cup sliced chestnut/cremini mushrooms
4 Swiss chard leaves, sliced
4 gluten-free corn tortillas
sea salt and black pepper, to season

SERVES 2

Whisk the eggs and milk together in a bowl and leave to one side.

Heat 1 tablespoon of the olive oil in a frying pan/skillet over low heat, add the onion and thyme and cook slowly for 6–7 minutes, so the onion starts to caramelize. Add the mushrooms and Swiss chard and cook, turning up the heat a little, for another 2–3 minutes, until the mushrooms have browned and the chard has wilted.

While the vegetables are cooking, you can start heating the tortillas in a separate frying pan/skillet or griddle pan. Without any oil, over medium heat, I simply add a tortilla and heat for 15 seconds each side. Wrap in foil and a kitchen cloth to keep warm.

Put the cooked vegetables into a separate bowl to the one with the egg mixture and return the pan to the heat. Add the remaining ½ tablespoon of olive oil to the pan and when hot pour in the egg mixture and a pinch of salt and pepper. Leave the eggs to settle on the bottom and then scramble them by stirring every now and then. Keep doing this until the eggs are just cooked through.

Spoon a couple of tablespoons of scrambled eggs onto each warm corn tortilla, then top with a tablespoon or two of the cooked vegetables. Garnish with a few extra thyme leaves, wrap up and eat straight away while still hot.

(E) (H) (M) (S) TURMERIC SCRAMBLED EGGS WITH SPINACH AND GHEE

Turmeric or 'haldi' in Indian culture has been used for centuries in skin and hair beauty regimes for its antibacterial and antioxidant properties. It is part of the ginger family and can be used raw or in powder form. Ground turmeric is widely used in face masks and even in pastes to heal wounds. The spice contains the active ingredient curcumin which is known to help prevent hair loss.

4 eggs
125 ml/½ cup soy milk or other milk of your choosing
1 tablespoon ghee
60–80 g/about ½ cup sliced onion, to taste
½ teaspoon ground turmeric
¼ teaspoon ground cumin
100 g/2 cups baby spinach leaves, well rinsed
sea salt and black pepper, to season

SERVES 2

Whisk the eggs and milk together in a bowl with a pinch of salt and pepper.

Heat the ghee in a large frying pan/skillet over low–medium heat. Add the onion, turmeric and cumin and cook until the onion slices are soft. Add the spinach and cook until the leaves are wilted.

Push the spinach and onions to one side and pour the eggs into the pan. Leave the eggs to settle on the bottom and then scramble them by stirring every now and then. Once they are nearly cooked through and firming up, stir in the spinach and onion mixture.

Serve up, piping hot.

Eggs

Eggs are great for your hair, skin and nails as well as providing many other great health benefits. The lutein keeps skin elastic and hydrated, and the protein helps repair skin tissues and keeps hair strong and shiny. Egg yolks are packed full of goodness, but most importantly contain essential fatty acids and fat soluble vitamins. The omega-3 content is needed for proper brain and eye retina functions, while the Omega-6s are essential for healthy skin, hair, good libido, the reproductive system and growth.

PAPAYA, RUBY RED GRAPEFRUIT AND RASPBERRY FRUIT SALAD

The papaya, or 'pawpaw' as it is commonly known around the world, is a fruit exceptionally good for your eye health, as well as being great for digestion, and skin protection. The ripe orange flesh is a great source of beta-carotene and also two phytonutrients called lutein and zeaxanthin, which are crucial for eye health and can help reduce the risk of age-related macular degeneration – a common cause of blindness. The grapefruit and raspberries are a fantastic source of vitamin C and antioxidants which are also critical to eye health.

1 ripe small papaya, peeled
1 ripe ruby red grapefruit, peeled
120 g/1 cup fresh raspberries
zest of 1 lime
1 tablespoon honey or agave syrup (optional)
lime wedges, to serve

SERVES 2–4

First, cut the papaya in half. Scoop out the seeds and pulp leaving just the flesh shell. Cut into bite-size cubes and put in a large bowl.

Cut the grapefruit segments from their skins and cut the flesh into bite-size cubes. Add to the bowl with the papaya.

Add the raspberries, lime zest and honey (if using) and give everything a good stir.

Serve straight up with a wedge of lime to squeeze over, or save some, cover and store in the fridge to have the next day.

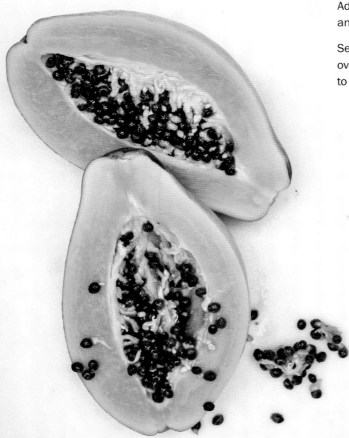

(E) (M) (S) GREEN EGGS, SPINACH AND AVOCADO WITH BASIL AND CORIANDER/CILANTRO DRESSING

Vitamins C and D play a crucial role in keeping the blood vessels that transport all the nutrients to our muscles healthy. Eggs are a great source of protein and also vitamin D. The cherry tomatoes have the vitamin C, and the spinach is an excellent source of calcium. Calcium helps the body to send signals to your muscles such as when to contract, and helps build muscle tone.

1 ripe hass avocado
80 g/½ cup cherry tomatoes
200 g/4 cups baby spinach leaves
4 eggs
½ teaspoon white wine or malt vinegar

BASIL AND CORIANDER/ CILANTRO DRESSING
25 g/½ cup fresh basil
10 g/¼ cup fresh coriander/cilantro
60 ml/¼ cup extra virgin olive oil
1 garlic clove
a pinch each of sea salt and black pepper

a high-speed blender

SERVES 2

First, half-fill a large saucepan with water and bring to the boil over medium heat.

Next, prepare the dressing. Simply add all the ingredients to a blender and whizz until smooth. Leave to one side.

Peel the avocado, remove the stone/pit and chop the flesh into small chunks. Cut the cherry tomatoes in half. Set aside.

Add the spinach to the hot water, leave it to wilt for about 30 seconds, then transfer to a bowl using a slotted spoon – you want to keep the water on the heat as you will use it to cook the eggs in (plus it saves washing up). Once the spinach has cooled a bit, squeeze out the excess water and set aside.

Next, poach the eggs. Add the vinegar to the pan with water, then crack the eggs, one by one, into the water. Get each egg as close to the simmering water as you can before gently cracking the shell to release the egg into the water slowly so it has a better chance of holding its shape. Cook for about 2 minutes, depending on how runny you like the yolks. You can lift the eggs from the water using a slotted spoon and gently touch the yolk to see if it is to your liking.

Arrange the wilted spinach, avocado chunks and cherry tomatoes on serving plates.

Using a slotted spoon, carefully remove the eggs, draining off as much water as possible – I use paper towels to dab the underneath of the spoon to get all the excess water. Lay the eggs on top of the vegetables, drizzle with the dressing, sprinkle with salt and pepper, and serve.

H D S PEANUT BUTTER, CHIA, OAT AND CHOCOLATE BREAKFAST COOKIES

I like to have a batch of these breakfast cookies at home to snack on with my daughter, because, being a working single mother I am always on the run. The oats and chia seeds are both excellent sources of dietary fibre, which aids digestion and eliminates toxins in the body, and the omega-3 fats found in peanuts are known to help with acne and wrinkles, keeping hair and nails strong and shiny. The chocolate also provides plenty of energy to keep you going.

185 g/¾ cup peanut butter
50 g/3½ tablespoons ghee
85 g/½ cup raw demerara/turbinado sugar
2 eggs
85 g/1 cup gluten-free oats or steel-cut oats
1 teaspoon bicarbonate of soda/baking soda

125 g/1 cup gluten-free plain/all-purpose flour
2 tablespoons chia seeds
85 g/½ cup dark/ bittersweet chocolate chips or pure cacao chips (70 per cent cocoa solids)

a baking sheet, lined with baking parchment

MAKES ABOUT 16

Preheat the oven 190°C (375°F) Gas 5.

Beat together the peanut butter, ghee and sugar in a large mixing bowl, until fluffy. Beat in the eggs, one at a time, then stir in the oats, bicarbonate of soda/baking soda, flour, chia seeds and chocolate chips. Bring the mixture together, then roll into balls with your hands. Arrange the balls on the prepared baking sheet and flatten them into cookie shapes with the palm of your hand. Pop into the preheated oven to bake for 15 minutes, until slightly golden.

Transfer to a wire rack to cool. Enjoy immediately or store in an airtight container for up to 7 days.

B S BREAKFAST FIGS WITH HONEY AND RASPBERRIES

This is a very easy breakfast to put together that is packed full of calcium and potassium to keep your bones in tip-top condition. The high amounts of potassium in the figs prevents the body from losing too much calcium in the urine, which happens if we have a high-salt diet. Figs are also a great source of fruit fibre and natural fruit sugars. I use a mixture of fresh and dried figs as the dried figs have a higher concentration of nutrients but the fresh figs add a different flavour and texture, which I love at breakfast time.

3 dried figs, chopped
120 g/1 cup fresh raspberries
2 fresh figs, sliced
25 g/¼ cup pistachios, chopped

25 g/¼ cup almonds, chopped
2 tablespoons honey
Greek yogurt, to serve

SERVES 2–4

Add the chopped dried figs and raspberries to a large mixing bowl and mash together with a fork. Swirl this into the Greek yogurt and serve in bowls.

Top with sliced fresh figs, a sprinkle of chopped pistachios and almonds, and lastly the honey.

Who doesn't like to snack? I've always been a food lover, it's why I became a chef, and I firmly believe that one of life's simple pleasures is to eat delicious and nutritious food. Eating real fresh foods is something to be savoured, enjoyed and to feel grateful for. Here is my selection of snacks and side dishes that I love to eat, knowing that they are all actually making me pretty while I nibble. Extra bonus!

Snacks and sides

ANCIENT GRAIN CRACKERS

D H S

Ancient grains are on the comeback for their high levels of plant-based proteins. In addition, they all retain higher amounts of minerals and nutrients than the highly processed grains more commonly used that have been stripped of most of their nutritional goodness.

125 g/1 cup spelt flour or gluten-free plain/all-purpose flour
65 g/½ cup milled flaxseeds/linseeds
4½ tablespoons ghee or butter

90 g/¾ cup mixed power seeds (hemp, chia, amaranth, sesame)
sea salt and black pepper, to season

a food processor

MAKES ABOUT 35

Put the flour, flaxseeds/linseeds and ghee into a food processor. Pulse to form breadcrumbs. Add 6 tablespoons of cold water and pulse again, until it forms large chunks. Tip into a bowl and add the mixed power seeds. Roll together to form a soft ball of dough. Put in the fridge to rest for 15–30 minutes. Preheat the oven to 190°C (375°F) Gas 5.

Cut the dough in half and place each piece between two sheets of baking parchment. Roll into a very thin layer using a rolling pin, to just below 3-mm/⅛-inch thick. The thinner the dough, the crispier the cracker. Take off the top layer of parchment, keeping the rolled dough on the bottom layer. Cut the dough into equal squares using a sharp knife or pastry cutter. Sprinkle with salt and pepper and carefully lift the parchment with the squares onto the baking sheets.

Bake in the preheated oven for 15–18 minutes, depending on how crunchy you like them. They will be golden-brown and firm when cooked. Leave to cool on the baking sheets, then serve. Store in an airtight container for up to 2 weeks.

KIDNEY BEAN DIP WITH FETA TOPPING

H

Your hair is constantly growing and so needs a regular supply of the nutrients that are essential to keep it strong and healthy. Kidney beans are part of the legume family which are a great source of protein, iron, biotin and zinc – all of which are key nutrients for luscious locks.

2 tablespoons olive oil
1 shallot, finely chopped
2 fat garlic cloves, finely chopped
1 celery stalk/rib, finely chopped
¼ teaspoon ground cumin
½ teaspoon paprika
a 420-g/15-oz. can of kidney beans, drained
1 tablespoon tomato purée/paste

2 tablespoons chopped fresh coriander/cilantro
1 tablespoon crumbled feta cheese
sea salt and black pepper, to season

a high-speed blender (optional)

MAKES 450 G/1 LB. AND SERVES 2–4

Heat the oil in a frying pan/skillet over low heat. Add the shallot, garlic and celery, then the cumin and paprika. Sauté for 3–4 minutes, until soft.

Add the kidney beans, 250 ml/1 cup of water and the tomato purée/paste. Leave to simmer gently for 15 minutes, giving it a stir every now and then. Add an extra tablespoon or two of water if it gets too dry. Once everything is soft, remove the pan from the heat, mush together with a fork or blend if you prefer a smooth consistency.

Season to taste with salt and pepper, and stir in the coriander/cilantro. Sprinkle with feta cheese immediately before serving and enjoy!

(M) VIETNAMESE CHICKEN AND QUINOA PROTEIN BITES

Exercise ultimately helps build muscle, but we have to make sure we get enough protein in our diets before and after exercise because it cannot be stored in our bodies for very long. Protein is needed to build healthy bones, cartilage, muscles, blood and skin, as well as many other functions in the body. The quinoa and chicken in this dish are packed full of proteins making these light bites a perfect high-protein snack. I like to freeze some after cooking and take a few out for lunchboxes.

85 g/½ cup quinoa
450 g/1 lb. ground chicken
½ teaspoon sea salt
1 tablespoon sweet chilli sauce, plus extra to serve
1 tablespoon cornflour/cornstarch
2 teaspoons sesame oil
2 tablespoons vegetable or coconut oil
lettuce leaves and fresh coriander/cilantro, to serve

SPICE PASTE
50 g/½ cup sliced shallots
20 g/½ cup fresh mint
20 g/½ cup fresh coriander/cilantro
2 lemongrass stalks, outer leaf discarded and roughly chopped
a 2.5-cm/1-inch piece of fresh ginger
3 garlic cloves
½ tablespoon fish sauce
2 Bird's eye chillies/chiles
1 tablespoon vegetable or coconut oil

a high-speed blender
a baking sheet lined with baking parchment

MAKES 20

Start by cooking the quinoa. Put it in a small saucepan and pour over 250 ml/1 cup of water. Set over medium heat and bring to the boil, then reduce the heat to low. Simmer with a lid on for 10 minutes, until the quinoa is soft and fluffy and all the water has been soaked up. Leave to one side to cool down.

Preheat the oven to 200°C (400°F) Gas 6.

Add all the ingredients for the spice paste to a blender and whizz until smooth. Transfer to a large mixing bowl.

Add the ground chicken to the spice paste, then the cooled quinoa, the salt, sweet chilli sauce and cornflour/cornstarch, and mix everything together.

Dampen your hands with water and roll the mixture into balls. I try to make them all about 1 tablespoon in size. Lay the balls on the prepared baking sheet and drizzle with both the sesame and vegetable oils.

Bake in the preheated oven for 10–15 minutes, depending on the size of your balls. Once cooked, they will be white all the way through – no pink bits inside – and slightly browned on the base. Cut one open to check it is cooked all the way through.

You can eat these straight away – I like to wrap mine in lettuce leaves with some fresh coriander/cilantro and sweet chilli sauce on the side to dip into. Or, you can keep them in the fridge for up to 2 days.

D ALGAE POPCORN WITH GHEE AND SEA SALT

Popcorn is a great source of insoluble fibre. Fibre is needed to help push the food along the digestive tract keeping you regular. Fibre does not actually get digested so make sure you don't overload your system as too much can also cause problems like gas and bloating if you have existing digestive problems. Popcorn is for sharing! Algae oil is a great vegetarian source of omega-3s and DHA fatty acids, which are essential for healthy brains. Spirulina is a blue-green algae with high levels of vitamins, phytonutrients and antioxidants. Such a delicious, healthy snack that takes less than 10 minutes to make, perfect for a movie night. Once you make your own popcorn you won't be able to stop!

60 ml/¼ cup algae oil
120 g/⅔ cup popcorn
    kernels
2 teaspoons spirulina
    powder

½–1 teaspoon fine sea
    salt, to taste
2 tablespoons ghee,
    melted

SERVES 4–5

Pour the algae oil into a large saucepan with a lid and add the corn kernels. Pop the lid on and set over medium heat until you start to hear the corn popping. Once you hear the popping, carefully shake the pan, holding onto the lid. The corn will keep popping for 2–3 minutes.

Take the pan off the heat and leave the lid on for a couple of minutes in case any kernels continue to pop. Take the lid off and sprinkle over the spirulina powder and salt, and toss together. Drizzle the melted ghee all over and toss the popcorn again, until everything is well mixed together.

Serve straight away – freshly made, warm popcorn is the best!

M SWEET SPICED MIXED NUTS

Nuts are great to have as a snack. They are a good source of non-animal protein and contain many good nutrients. Eating a handful of nuts or other protein sources after a workout can help with muscle growth.

250 g/2 cups mixed raw
    nuts
2 tablespoons honey or
    agave syrup
½ teaspoon ground
    ginger
1 teaspoon ground
    cinnamon

2 tablespoons coconut
    sugar or raw brown
    sugar
¼ teaspoon sea salt
    (optional)

*a baking sheet lined with
    baking parchment and
    brushed with olive oil*

SERVES 4

Preheat the oven to 180°C (350°F) Gas 4.

Put the nuts in a large mixing bowl and add the honey and spices. Mix well to coat, then spread the nuts onto the prepared baking sheet. Pop into the preheated oven for 8–10 minutes.

While the nuts are in the oven, put the sugar and salt into a clean bowl. As soon as the nuts come out of the oven, spoon them into the bowl of sugar and salt and toss them around to coat evenly.

Spread them out onto a sheet of baking parchment so they don't clump together, and leave to cool.

Nibble as a healthy sweet treat, perfect for mid-afternoon sugar cravings. Store in an airtight container for up to 2 weeks.

Algae oil

Algae oil is a great vegetarian source of DHAs and essential fatty acids found most commonly in fish. Said to help reduce inflammatory conditions such as IBS, improve memory, heart functionality and brain health, adding a drop of this wonder-oil will make a big difference to the way you feel.

B LEMON, TARRAGON AND SARDINE PÂTÉ

I think sardines are very under-used and often underrated. These small, affordable fish are a rich source of vitamin D, which helps calcium to be absorbed to nourish our bones. They are also a rich source of calcium, vitamins B12 and phosphorous, which all help strengthen our bone matrix.

2 tablespoons olive oil
½ red onion, sliced
1½ tablespoons chopped fresh tarragon leaves
2 x 120-g/3¾-oz. cans of sardines in water, drained
a pinch each of sea salt and black pepper
zest and juice of 1 lemon
2 tablespoons ghee, melted

TO SERVE
toast or Ancient Grain Crackers (page 60)
1 cucumber, sliced
fresh tarragon leaves
lemon wedges

a food processor

SERVES 4

Heat the olive oil in a frying pan/skillet over low–medium heat. Add the red onion and cook for 6–7 minutes, until the onion softens and begins to caramelize. Add the tarragon near the end and cook for another minute. Leave to cool slightly, then transfer to a food processor.

Add the sardines, salt and pepper, lemon zest and juice and melted ghee. (There is no need to pick the tiny bones out of the sardines as they will be blended and provide extra calcium.) Blend until you have a smooth pâté.

This is delicious spread on toast or crackers with a few slices of cucumber on top. Serve sprinkled with tarragon leaves and lemon wedges on the side to squeeze.

Store in an airtight container in the fridge for 3–4 days.

ⒽⒹ BLACK SALSIFY MASH

Some studies have shown that the leading cause of hair-loss in pre-menopausal women is a lack of iron. Salsify is a winter root and super-tuber, a highly nutritious vegetable, that is particularly good for hair growth as it contains high levels of iron, copper and also vitamin C. Iron is needed by the body to carry oxygen in the blood to the scalp. Copper is known for keeping the greys at bay and maintaining hair strength as well as promoting hair growth. Vitamin C aids the absorption of iron and is needed for the formation of collagen which keeps our hair follicles strong. So, when salsify is in season, be sure to grab a bunch to cook with.

300 g/10½ oz. black salsify root

1 tablespoon chopped fresh flat-leaf parsley (optional)

1 tablespoon butter or ghee

sea salt and black pepper, to season

a large bowl filled with water and ½ lemon squeezed in

SERVES 2

Peel the skin off the salsify and chop the flesh into 2.5-cm/1-inch pieces. Add the salsify to the prepared citrus water bowl as you prepare them. Leave to sit in the citrus water for 5 minutes – this helps to stop discolouration.

Drain the salsify, then put in a saucepan. Cover with water and set over medium heat to boil for 10–15 minutes, until soft.

Drain and return to the pan or a large mixing bowl. Sprinkle over the chopped parsley, add the butter and season with salt and pepper. Using a fork, roughly mash the salsify – you can make this as smooth or chunky as you like.

Serve hot as a delicious and healthy side dish.

Ⓗ ROASTED COCONUT CAULIFLOWER

The mighty cauliflower is packed full of essential vitamins and nutrients as well as antioxidants, and it is also known for promoting healthy hair growth and skin due to the presence of sulphur and silicone.

2 tablespoons coconut flour

a small pinch of sea salt

1 teaspoon curry powder

½ cauliflower, cut into florets

1 tablespoon coconut oil

a baking sheet lined with baking parchment

SERVES 2

Preheat the oven to 200°C (400°F) Gas 6.

Put the coconut flour, salt and curry powder into a large mixing bowl. Stir, then add the cauliflower florets and toss so everything is evenly coated.

Spread the cauliflower onto the prepared baking sheet, dot the coconut oil around and pop into the preheated oven for 15 minutes.

Take out, turn the cauliflower and pop back into the oven for another 15–20 minutes, until the cauliflower has crisped up. Serve straight away.

Parsley

This fresh herb is packed full of vitamins and minerals, and has been known to help detoxify the body by flushing out excess liquids and supporting kidney function.

E CRISPY SWEET POTATO FRIES

S COCONUT
D AIOLI

Apart from being delicious, sweet potatoes contain an excellent supply of beta-carotene, essential for healthy, bright eyes. They also contain high levels of anthocyanin, which helps fight pigmentation and is an anti-inflammatory, and so is beneficial to the skin. They also contain a whole host of other vitamins and minerals, meaning there's no reason not to indulge in these delicious fries.

Coconut oil is used as part of a daily external beauty regime for a host of top celebs. It's full of antibacterial, anti-inflammatory, antioxidant and hydrating properties. It replenishes the skin's natural oils, keeping skin moisturized and soft. This aioli can be served alongside all manner of things to dip into, spread on sandwiches and drizzled over salads, so let the coconut do its thing from the inside out.

2 sweet potatoes
1 tablespoon cornflour/
  cornstarch
1 teaspoon sea salt
a pinch of black pepper
1–2 pinches of cayenne
  pepper or dried chilli/
  red pepper flakes
  (optional)

2 tablespoons coconut
  oil, melted
Coconut Aioli (right),
  to serve

*a baking sheet lined with
  baking parchment*

SERVES 2

1 large egg yolk
½ teaspoon Dijon
  mustard
2 teaspoons freshly
  squeezed lemon juice
60 ml/¼ cup light olive
  oil

60 ml/¼ cup organic
  unrefined virgin
  coconut oil, melted
2 garlic cloves, crushed

SERVES 2

NOTE As this recipe yields a small serving, I whisk by hand using a whisk and a bowl. Make sure the coconut oil is liquid and not solid. It should be melted but at room temperature.

Preheat the oven to its highest setting – 220°C (425°F) Gas 7.

Wash and scrub the sweet potatoes thoroughly. (I like to keep the skin on mine as it adds more fibre.) Cut the sweet potatoes into even-size fries and pop into a bowl. Sprinkle over the cornflour/cornstarch, salt, black pepper and cayenne pepper (if you like a little spice), then toss together making sure all the fries are well coated.

Spread the fries out evenly on the prepared baking sheet and pour over the melted coconut oil.

Pop into the preheated oven for 15 minutes. Take out and give them a turn, then return to the oven for another 10–15 minutes, until crisp.

Serve hot with coconut aioli on the side and sprinkled with extra cayenne pepper if desired.

Put the egg yolk, Dijon mustard and lemon juice into a mixing bowl and whisk together. Very slowly, add a couple of drops of the olive oil and whisk in. Repeat until it begins to come together and gets firmer. With practice, you can add the oil in a thin drizzle, whisking all the time.

Slowly add the melted coconut oil and keep whisking until it is all incorporated. Stir in the crushed garlic and serve.

Ⓜ WARM CHICKPEA AND SPINACH SALAD

Chickpeas, otherwise known as 'garbanzo beans' are high in fibre and protein. They also contain choline, which aids muscle movement, the structure of cellular membranes, and nerve impulses. Combined with iron-rich spinach, which also contains nitrates, they help to make muscles stronger. This salad provides a tasty and nutritious side or main meal.

2 tablespoons olive oil
1 garlic clove, crushed
¼ teaspoon ground cumin
¼ teaspoon dried thyme or ½ teaspoon fresh thyme leaves
a 400-g/14-oz. can of chickpeas, drained
100 g/2 cups baby spinach
3 tablespoons roughly chopped fresh flat-leaf parsley
zest of 1 lemon
2 tablespoons finely chopped red onion

TAHINI DRESSING
2 tablespoons tahini
2 tablespoons olive oil
juice of 1 lemon
a pinch each of sea salt and black pepper

SERVES 2–4

First, make the dressing. Simply stir all the ingredients together in a bowl with 1 tablespoon of water. (It helps sometimes to give the tahini a really good stir in the pot so it becomes a bit runny.)

Heat the olive oil in a large frying pan/skillet over low–medium heat. Add the garlic, cumin and thyme, and cook together for 30 seconds. Add the chickpeas, reduce the heat to low and continue to cook for 5 minutes. Add 2 tablespoons of water and leave to cook for another 3 minutes. I like to squash the chickpeas a little while they are cooking.

Lastly, stir in the spinach, chopped parsley, lemon zest and red onion.

Pour the tahini dressing over the top and toss together. Serve as a side or main meal.

Chickpeas

Also known as 'garbanzo beans', chickpeas are a complex carbohydrate from the legume family that are both high in protein and fibre. As a plant-based protein, they replace the need for added meat or fish and can be used to create a variety of vegetarian and vegan meals. Rich in iron, they help to keep muscles strong and healthy, and the fibre, as ever, aids digestion.

D KIMCHI

Fermented vegetables are well-known for aiding digestion. They contain high levels of probiotic bacteria and this Korean side dish has been used for medicinal purposes for centuries. It deserves its place amongst other beauty foods. Kimchi is a personal thing and so if you like it really spicy just add more pepper, if you like it less spicy add less, then ferment it for as long as you like. It takes a bit of experimenting and trying out of different vegetables to see what you like best.

½ napa cabbage
2 tablespoons sea salt
3 spring onions/scallions
1 carrot, thinly sliced
120 g/¾ cup sliced daikon radish
3 garlic cloves, finely grated
a 2.5-cm/1-inch piece of fresh ginger, finely grated
½ teaspoon caster/granulated sugar
2 tablespoons gochugaru (Korean red pepper powder)
1½ tablespoons fish sauce or shrimp paste (optional)

a 450-g/1-lb. capacity sterilized glass jar with airtight lid

SERVES 6–8

NOTE There are a few stages to this recipe, as it takes time for the fermentation process to work.

Start by washing the cabbage and cutting it into about 2.5-cm/1-inch thick pieces. Pop it all into a bowl, add the salt and rub it into the cabbage with your hands. Cover the cabbage with about 500 ml/2 cups of water. Cover loosely with clingfilm/plastic wrap and place something heavy on top to press it down. I use a small plate with a can of beans on top. Leave this to sit for an hour.

Drain the cabbage and rinse a few times to wash all the salt out. Gently squeeze out as much water as you can with your hands. Return the cabbage to the bowl and add the spring onions/scallions, carrot and daikon radish.

Put the garlic and ginger, sugar, gochugaru and fish sauce (if using) in a separate small bowl with 2 tablespoons of water. Stir until everything comes together, then pour over the vegetables and mix well.

Pop the vegetables into the jar and squish them down so you see the juices rising to the top. Screw the lid on and leave it to stand at room temperature for 1–5 days. The longer you leave it the more fermented and potent it will become – you should taste the kimchi after 1 day to see how it is developing and leave until the taste is to your liking.

Once fermented to your taste, you can then keep it in the fridge for up to 3 months in a sealed jar and take out a serving every time you want to eat it – kimchi is a great accompaniment to many meals. The longer it is left in the fridge, the more sour it will become – I like mine after 2–3 weeks. If it turns cloudy and the vegetables are like mush, the kimchi has turned bad and should be thrown out.

This chapter features a whole host of
my favourite salads and soups that I eat
regularly. The great thing is you can make
large batches of both that will keep in the
fridge or freezer and you can take leftovers
into work to have for lunch the next day.
Each recipe is specifically created for either
skin, hair, eyes, bones, digestion or muscle
health, and they are packed full of the
essential nutrients needed for each area.
Mix and match these dishes to get a well-
balanced, inside-job beauty food makeover.

Soups and small plates

S H B BONE BROTH

There is a lot of truth in the old saying, 'chicken soup for the soul'. Bone broth is known as one of the oldest healing and anti-aging remedies on the planet. You can make bone broths from all bones but my preferences are chicken, beef, and fish. The newest, natural anti-aging beauty secret of many of Hollywood's top celebrities is to drink a cup of bone broth every day for youthful skin, healthy hair and nails, plus good bone and joint health. This beef bone broth is a potent source of collagen, glycine and many other beauty-boosting minerals.

1.3–1.8 kg/3–4 lb. beef bones (use a mixture of marrow, short ribs, knuckles, etc.)
½ leek, roughly chopped
1 small onion, quartered
3 carrots, roughly chopped
2 fresh or dried bay leaves
2 garlic cloves
1 teaspoon black peppercorns

MAKES 1 LITRE/4 CUPS

Preheat the oven to 190°C (375°F) Gas 5.

This is very easy to make, it takes a long time, but is well worth it. Start by popping the bones into a roasting pan, then put in the preheated oven to roast for 30 minutes. This enhances the flavour. Remove from the oven, put the bones into a large saucepan and scrape all of the juices on the bottom of the pan in, too.

Add 2 litres/3½ pints of water and all the remaining ingredients. Bring to the boil over medium heat, then turn down to low and simmer, covered, for a minimum of 8 hours. The longer you simmer the broth, the stronger and more potent the nutritional benefits will be.

Strain the broth through a fine-mesh sieve or strainer and discard the bones, vegetables and flavourings. Leave to cool, then keep in an airtight container in the fridge for up to 2 days. Once it chills, the consistency will turn gelatinous because of the high level of gelatine that has seeped from the bones. It is a good reminder of the benefits of this broth and its ability to keep the skin plump and elastic.

To serve, scrape off the top layer of fat and discard. Reheat and enjoy, or add to stocks and sauces.

NOTE You can divide the broth into portions and freeze for up to 2 months.

Ⓗ Ⓢ GORGEOUS
Ⓓ GREEN SOUP

Spinach has high levels of vitamin A and iron which are both said to be important for healthy skin, hair and nails. This vegan and gluten-free soup has a mixture of only green vegetables, a great source of fibre to help your digestive system and keep you regular, and is blended with coconut oils and milk for those good, skin-loving fats.

250 g/2 cups frozen peas
2 tablespoons coconut oil
4 garlic cloves, roughly chopped
1 leek, roughly chopped
½ head of broccoli, roughly chopped
200 g/4 cups baby spinach
1–1.25 litres/4–5 cups organic vegetable stock

a big handful of fresh parsley, plus extra chopped to garnish
60 ml/¼ cup coconut cream
sea salt and black pepper, to season

a food processor

SERVES 4

First, cook the peas in a pan of boiling water for 2 minutes. Drain and leave to one side.

Heat the coconut oil in a large frying pan/skillet over low heat. Add the garlic, leek and broccoli, and sauté gently for 5 minutes. Add 2 tablespoons of water and pop a lid onto the pan to gently steam the broccoli to soften it.

Transfer half of the cooked veggies from the pan to a food processor, add half of the peas and half of the spinach, then blend. Add half of the vegetable stock, parsley and coconut cream, and whizz until smooth. Pour the mixture into a saucepan and then repeat with the remaining ingredients.

Combine both blended mixtures in the saucepan and warm gently over low–medium heat. Season to taste, then serve warm, garnished with chopped fresh parsley.

Ⓔ SPICY BUTTERNUT
Ⓢ SQUASH SOUP

This beta-carotene-packed soup is perfect for keeping your eyes bright, shiny and in good health. Beta-carotene is converted to vitamin A in the body, which is essential for your vision and helps the eye retina function properly. A study published by the American 'Journal of Agriculture and Food Chemistry' in 2002 said that cooking beta-carotene-rich vegetables like carrots actually increases the levels of beta-carotene, so whizz up a bowl of this spicy soup to get your eyes shining.

2 tablespoons olive oil or coconut oil
1 small onion, roughly chopped
3 garlic cloves, chopped
a 5-cm/2-inch piece of fresh ginger, roughly chopped
1–2 fresh red chillies/ chiles, sliced
1 teaspoon ground cumin
2 teaspoons ground coriander
1 small butternut squash, peeled, deseeded and cubed

3 carrots, peeled and cubed, plus extra peeled strips to garnish
½ sweet potato, peeled and cubed
2 litres/3½ pints organic vegetable stock
20 g/½ cup fresh coriander/cilantro, plus extra to garnish
60 ml/¼ cup coconut cream
sea salt and black pepper, to season

a food processor

SERVES 4

Heat the oil in a large saucepan over medium heat. Add the onion, garlic, ginger, chillies/chiles, ground cumin and ground coriander, and cook for 2 minutes. Add the squash, carrots, sweet potato and stock, and leave to simmer, uncovered, for 30 minutes. Turn off the heat and leave to cool.

Blend everything with the fresh coriander/cilantro, including the coconut cream until smooth. Return to the pan, reheat, season and serve piping hot. Garnish with extra chilli/chile, peeled carrot and coriander/cilantro.

D MAGICAL MISO SOUP

Miso paste is a Japanese fermented soy bean paste, which is also a probiotic that can help with digestive problems. It is a great source of B-vitamins, calcium, iron, zinc, copper and magnesium, and my all-time favourite umami flavour!

½ block firm silken tofu
1 litre/4 cups dashi (Japanese stock, see Note)
4 tablespoons dark miso paste
1 tablespoon dried seaweed
2 spring onions/ scallions, thinly sliced

SERVES 2

First, drain the tofu and wrap in a few layers of paper towels. Put something heavy on top (a can of beans or similar) for 10 minutes to help press out any excess water.

Meanwhile, very gently heat the dashi in a saucepan over low heat – you don't want it to boil! Once it's warm, mix a few tablespoons of the stock into the miso paste in a large mixing bowl. Once smooth, pour it back into the pan with the remaining dashi and stir together.

Unwrap the tofu and chop or break into pieces.

Add the seaweed, tofu and spring onions/scallions to the pan. Heat gently until hot but not boiling.

Serve hot.

NOTE Dashi is simply made from boiling kelp, water and bonito flakes together, but is readily available in Asian or health food stores.

B M JAPANESE SPINACH WITH SESAME SEED DRESSING

Spinach is an excellent source of calcium which is vital for strong bones and teeth. The Popeye theme song always comes into my head when I think of spinach, because it really does make you strong. This recipe is one of my favourite ways of eating this powerful green leaf.

300 g/6 cups spinach
4 tablespoons white sesame seeds
2 tablespoons soy sauce
2 teaspoons honey or agave syrup
a food processor

SERVES 2

NOTE Wash the spinach thoroughly as spinach has a tendency to hold lots of grit.

Fill a medium-size saucepan with water. Bring to a boil over medium heat and pop in the spinach for no more than 30 seconds to wilt. Drain the spinach, and immediately immerse in cold water to stop it cooking any more – this helps to keep its green colour. Squeeze out as much water as you can and set aside.

To make the dressing, put the sesame seeds in a small frying pan/skillet and cook over low heat until they start to brown. Make sure you keep an eye on them as they burn easily. Once lightly golden and smelling fantastic, transfer the seeds to a bowl to cool slightly. Once cool, add the sesame seeds, soy sauce and honey to a food processor and blend until you have a rough paste. (You can also do this using a pestle and mortar if preferred.)

Add the paste to the spinach, stir through and serve.

SHAVED BRUSSELS SALAD WITH ALMONDS AND INCA BERRIES

This salad is a super-charged blend of natural antioxidants, vitamins C, A and E – a true boost of what your skin needs to glow. Who knew these small green balls of goodness (that most of us hated when we were young) would turn out to be one of the most nutritious vegetables around? Brussels sprouts are packed full of antioxidants, flavonoids, vitamins, minerals and selenium. They are also a rich source of vitamin C, which is essential for the formation of collagen, the main support system of our skin. Vitamin C also helps fight against skin damage, and keeps our skin plump and the wrinkles at bay. Inca berries (also known as 'golden berries' or 'physalis') are a South American super-fruit treasure. Packed full of vitamins C, A and B12 and antioxidants, and high in bioflavonoids, they have been used for centuries for healing, detoxifying and energizing. The almonds in this salad contain a good amount of vitamin E and healthy fats essential for keeping the skin looking young and for the prevention of cell damage.

400 g/4 cups Brussels
    sprouts, thinly sliced
80 g/1 cup flaked/
    slivered almonds,
    toasted
70 g/½ cup inca/golden
    berries
70 g/½ cup sliced red
    onion

DRESSING
juice of 1 lemon
125 ml/½ cup olive oil
a pinch each of sea salt
    and black pepper
1 teaspoon Dijon
    mustard
2 tablespoons honey

SERVES 2

Start by making the dressing. Add all the ingredients to a clean jar, screw on the lid and shake well to mix. Alternatively, whisk everything together in a small bowl until well combined.

Put all of the salad ingredients into a large mixing bowl and pour the dressing over, toss together and serve.

ⓢ ROASTED BEETROOT/BEET, RED QUINOA,
ⓜ STRAWBERRY AND BASIL SALAD

Beetroot/beets are well-known for improving complexion, dry skin, acne-prone skin and even for helping keep hair thick and shiny. This is largely due to the high amounts of folate they contain, as well as the vitamin C, vitamin B6, manganese, betaine and potassium. In this salad, I use the beetroot/beet green tops too as they are not to be discarded! It is said that the tops are packed with even more nutrition than the vegetable itself, containing high levels of calcium, iron and vitamins A and C, plus they actually taste great!

3 medium raw mixed purple and golden beetroot/beets (including the tops)
2 tablespoons honey
2 tablespoons balsamic vinegar
2 tablespoons olive oil
3 sprigs of fresh thyme
170 g/1 cup red quinoa
150 g/1½ cups fresh strawberries, trimmed and sliced
2 small handfuls of fresh basil leaves
100 g/½ cup crumbled goat's cheese
edible flowers, to garnish

DRESSING
3 tablespoons balsamic vinegar
3 tablespoons olive oil
1 garlic clove, finely chopped
1 tablespoon strawberry jam/jelly
1 tablespoon wholegrain mustard
a pinch each of sea salt and black pepper

a baking sheet lined with foil

SERVES 4-6

Preheat the oven to 190°C (375°F) Gas 5.

Start by roasting the beetroot/beets. Cut off the tops and bottoms, reserving the tops. Give the beetroot/beets a good scrub and then cut into quarters. Spread out on the prepared baking sheet, drizzle over 2 tablespoons of water, the honey, balsamic vinegar and olive oil, and scatter over the thyme. Fold up the sides of the foil so that the beetroot/beets are covered. Pop into the preheated oven and roast for 50 minutes. They should now be soft all the way through if you poke them with a knife. Remove from the oven and leave to cool. Once cooled slightly, peel off the outer skins.

Wash the beetroot/beet tops thoroughly to get rid of any grit and chop the leaves finely. You will need about 2 handfuls of chopped leaves.

To cook the quinoa, just put it in a saucepan with 500 ml/2 cups of water, bring to the boil, then turn the heat down to a gentle simmer. Put a lid on the pan and leave to cook for 10–12 minutes, or until the water has been absorbed. Leave to cool.

To make the dressing, simply add all the ingredients to a clean jar, screw on the lid and shake well to mix. Alternatively, whisk everything together in a small bowl until well combined.

Once everything has cooled down, you can assemble the salad. Put the quinoa, beetroot/beets, strawberries, beetroot/beet tops and dressing into a large mixing bowl and toss together. Sprinkle with basil and goat's cheese. I love to serve this salad with some edible flowers sprinkled on top – it makes a really beautiful centrepiece for a summer party.

SPIRULINA GREEN CHICKEN SALAD

Chicken is an excellent source of lean protein which helps muscle growth and repair, making this salad an excellent way to repair tired arms and legs after a tough workout. It also contains an amino acid called 'tryptophan,' which increases the serotonin levels in your brain, relieving stress and enhancing your mood. Add that to the natural endorphines generated by exercise and you'll have a potent combination of things to make you smile. Chicken also contains phosphorous, which helps aid bone and teeth structure.

2 chicken breasts
sesame oil, to drizzle
3 spring onions/scallions,
    finely chopped
2 tablespoons chopped
    fresh coriander/
    cilantro
2 tablespoons chopped
    fresh mint
2 tablespoons dried fried
    onions
2 tablespoons toasted
    sesame seeds
cooked brown rice or
    a mixed green salad,
    to serve

DRESSING
4 tablespoons freshly
    squeezed lime juice
1 teaspoon spirulina
    powder
1 tablespoon fish sauce
1 tablespoon finely
    chopped fresh ginger
2 tablespoons sweet
    chilli sauce

SERVES 2

Preheat the oven to 180°C (350°F) Gas 4.

Drizzle the chicken breasts with sesame oil, then wrap loosely in foil. Put on a baking sheet and bake in the preheated oven for 15–20 minutes, until cooked through. Cool slightly, then pull the meat apart with your fingers to shred it and put in a large mixing bowl.

Add the spring onions/scallions, fresh coriander/cilantro, fresh mint, dried fried onions and sesame seeds to the chicken and toss together.

In a separate small bowl, whisk all the dressing ingredients together. Drizzle over the chicken salad and mix together, then serve with either cooked brown rice or a big green salad.

Spirulina

Spirulina is a blue-green algae that is said to be one of the most nutritious and nutritionally concentrated food sources. It is a true powerhouse of multivitamins, minerals and fatty acids. Its super-high level of amino acids, vitamin A, essential fatty acids and beta-carotene can be easily used by the body to help support growth. It is the healthy fat called 'GLA' found in spirulina that is particularly good for keeping your hair shiny and lush, as well as your skin clear. I find adding a teaspoon of spirulina to many dishes or morning smoothies is a brilliant way to feed your body what it needs so you can glow inside and out.

CARROT, PARSNIP, FETA AND WALNUT CAKES

H **E**

Biotin is the part of B-complex vitamins that is responsible for a boost in hair growth as well as many other functions in the body. A biotin deficiency is known to cause unhealthy skin, weak nails and hair loss. It is a water-soluble vitamin, meaning the body cannot hold onto it for long, so we need to make sure we replenish our supplies regularly. Carrots and walnuts are a great natural source of biotin, so try these super-simple pan-fried cakes.

3 medium carrots, grated

2 medium parsnips, grated

1 small onion, thinly sliced

100 g/¾ cup brown rice flour

70 g/½ cup walnut pieces, chopped

1 egg

100 g/1 cup cubed feta

2–3 tablespoons coconut oil or oil of your choice, for cooking

sea salt and black pepper, to season

TO SERVE (OPTIONAL)

thinly sliced fresh vegetables

olive oil, to drizzle

fresh dill fronds

MAKES ABOUT 8 CAKES AND SERVES 4

These delicious savoury cakes are so simple to make. Put all of the ingredients, apart from the feta and oil, into a large mixing bowl. Add a big pinch each of salt and pepper, and mix together – using your hands is the best way! Add the feta last and mix in.

Roll a couple of spoonfuls of the mixture into round patties with your hands and place on a baking sheet or plate ready to cook. Repeat, then, once you have used up all the mixture, heat a tablespoon of oil in a large frying pan/skillet over medium heat. When hot, carefully lay the patties in the pan and cook for 2–3 minutes on each side. You may need to do this in batches depending on the size of your pan, adding extra oil to the pan each time. Keep the heat on medium and not too hot, or they will burn before cooking all the way through.

When the cakes are golden and crispy but still soft in the middle, they are ready to serve.

I like to serve two cakes per person with a side of thinly sliced vegetables. Season with salt and pepper, drizzle with a little oil and sprinkle with fresh dill fronds. Enjoy.

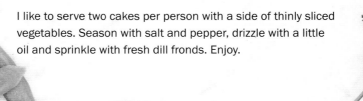

S E TUNA AND SPINACH SALAD

This is my version of my favourite French salad, the Niçoise. I've changed just a few ingredients to pack this tasty salad with ingredients that contain all the nutrients your eyes need to stay healthy. Spinach is full of carotenoids, antioxidants that help prevent macular degeneration, and both spinach and egg yolks are a great source of two other antioxidants, lutein and zeaxanthin, which help lower the risk of cataracts. DHA fatty acids are essential to eye health and are found in the anchovies and tuna. While the carrots contain beta-carotene for proper retina function.

2 fresh tuna steaks
olive oil, for rubbing
150–200 g/3–4 cups
    baby spinach
2 hard-boiled/cooked
    eggs, peeled and
    sliced into quarters
200 g/7 oz. cooked new
    potatoes, sliced
140 g/1 cup cooked
    green/French beans
135 g/1 cup grated
    carrots
8–10 black olives,
    depending on size
8 canned anchovies
sea salt and black
    pepper, to season

FRENCH DRESSING
1 tablespoon Dijon or
    wholegrain mustard
1 tablespoon honey or
    caster/granulated
    sugar
3 tablespoons white wine
    vinegar
6 tablespoons olive oil
1 garlic clove, finely
    chopped
½ teaspoon sea salt

SERVES 2

First, make the dressing by simply adding all the ingredients to a clean jar, screw on the lid and shake well to mix. Alternatively, whisk everything together in a small bowl until well combined. You can make a larger batch and keep this stored in the fridge for up to 2 weeks.

Rub the tuna with a little olive oil and season with salt and pepper. Set a griddle pan or frying pan/skillet over medium heat until hot, then lay the tuna in the pan to cook for 1–2 minutes on each side. This is a light cook, so if you prefer the tuna to be well-cooked, simply cook on each side for a little longer.

Heap the spinach leaves onto serving plates, with the eggs, slices of potato, green/French beans, grated carrots, olives and anchovies. Lay the tuna steaks on top and drizzle with some French dressing to serve.

NOTE You could slice the tuna steaks and heap the ingredients into one big serving dish to share out at the table.

Tuna

Tuna is a great source of selenium which is needed to support elastin in the skin which enables firmness and tightness. DHA fatty acids are the primary oil in fish and it has been linked with helping prevent age-related macular degeneration in eyes.

Ⓔ SWEET POTATO, SPINACH AND RED ONION FRITTATA

Sweet potatoes are firstly delicious, but are also an excellent source of beta-carotene. Beta-carotene is converted to vitamin A in the body, which plays an important role in eye health by helping protect the surface of the eye, the cornea and surrounding mucous membranes. Combined with spinach and eggs here, this frittata will take really good care of your eyes.

1 sweet potato, peeled and sliced into 1-cm/½-inch rounds
150 g/3 cups baby spinach leaves
1–2 tablespoons olive oil, for frying
1 red onion, sliced
2 garlic cloves, finely chopped
½ teaspoon ground turmeric
6 eggs
sea salt and black pepper, to season
a side salad, to serve (optional)

SERVES 4–6

Put the sweet potato slices in a saucepan and cover with water. Bring to the boil over medium heat, then reduce the heat and leave to simmer for 7–8 minutes, or until soft all the way through. Drain and put in a bowl.

Put the spinach in a saucepan of boiling water and cook for about 30 seconds, until wilted. Drain and rinse with cold water to suspend the cooking. Squeeze out any excess water when cool enough to handle, then add to the sweet potatoes.

Heat a little olive oil in an ovenproof frying pan/skillet over low heat, add the onion, garlic and turmeric, and fry gently for 3–4 minutes, until the onion is soft. Add the onions to the sweet potato slices and gently fold everything together.

Add a little more olive oil to the same pan, whisk together the eggs with a pinch of salt and pepper, and pour one-third of it into the pan to create a layer of egg on the bottom. Wait for it to settle and cook slightly, then spoon the sweet potato mixture on top, followed by the rest of the eggs. Push the vegetables down so they're just about covered by the eggs and leave to cook for 2 minutes, still on low heat.

Preheat a grill/broiler to medium–hot.

Put the pan under the grill/broiler to finish cooking the frittata for about 5 minutes. You will know it is cooked all the way through when it doesn't wobble in the middle. You can also push the top with a knife and if you see runny egg it needs more time.

Once cooked all the way through, leave the frittata to sit in the pan for 5 minutes. Slice and serve up warm with a side salad if you like. This frittata is also delicious served cold, and great in a packed lunch.

ⓜ ADZUKI BEAN AND MUSHROOM POWER FALAFEL

These falafel are a super-charged plant-based source of protein, iron and vitamin D. The little, red adzuki bean is a Chinese superfood with an exceptionally high protein content. It is a great source of fibre and slow-releasing carbohydrate, it's low in fat, as well as a good source of iron and other vitamins and minerals. These mighty (but mini!) beans are also easier to digest than some other beans. I grew up using adzuki beans mainly in my Chinese-inspired desserts at home. My mother's favourite was the crispy pancakes I used to pan-fry with a mushy sweet filling of the red beans! The mushrooms here are a good source of vitamin D, which is encourages contractions, strength and growth in muscles. This dish is a great light lunch.

90 g/½ cup dried adzuki beans
1 small onion, quartered
2 garlic cloves
4 chestnut/crimini mushrooms
3 tablespoons fresh flat-leaf parsley
140 g/1 cup cooked chickpeas
1½ teaspoons ground cumin
1 teaspoon sea salt
3 tablespoons spelt or plain/all-purpose flour
3 tablespoons olive oil

TO SERVE
5 pitta breads
hoummus, to taste
chopped fresh tomatoes
¼ red onion, thinly sliced
¼ cucumber, finely diced
a bunch of salad leaves
feta cheese, crumbled

a food processor
a non-stick baking sheet

SERVES 5

To cook the adzuki beans, put them in a small saucepan and cover with 1.25 litres/5 cups of water and a lid. Set over low heat and simmer for 1½ hours, until soft. Drain off the excess liquid and set aside.

Put the onion, garlic, mushrooms and parsley in a food processor and pulse until everything is finely chopped. Add the adzuki beans, chickpeas, cumin, salt and flour, and pulse again until it all comes together and is roughly ground although not puréed – you want to keep a bit of texture.

Preheat the oven to 200°C (400°F) Gas 6.

Roll the mixture into about 20 balls with your hands – I try to use 1 tablespoon of the mixture per ball. Arrange on the non-stick baking sheet and drizzle with olive oil, then pop into the preheated oven for 25 minutes, turning once, halfway through. The falafels will crisp up on the outside and stay soft and fluffy in the middle. (You can, if you want, deep-fry these falafels, but I think they taste super-delicious oven-roasted, and it saves on the calories too!)

To serve, stuff the falafels into pitta breads with a dollop of hoummus. Mix together the tomatoes, red onion, cucumber and salad leaves, then add the feta cheese. Add this to the pitta breads too and enjoy!

NOTE To shorten the cooking time, soak the adzuki beans and chickpeas overnight if you're using them fresh. It's hard to find adzuki beans pre-cooked in cans so I just boil them myself. I also boil my own chickpeas, as I have a big bag of them, but canned organic chickpeas are absolutely fine to use!

ᴰ ARTICHOKE, COURGETTE/ZUCCHINI, PEA, KEFIR CHEESE AND MINT FRITTATA

Kefir is a potent form of probiotic and its health benefits for digestive problems are quite incredible. Some say it is the new, more powerful probiotic yogurt! Kefir is a fermented drink made from milk and cultures of yeast and lactic acid bacteria. It can help with intestinal and gut issues such as gas, bloating and increasing bowel movements. It also provides a wealth of proteins, vitamins and minerals.

2 tablespoons algae oil or olive oil

½ red onion, sliced

2 garlic cloves, finely chopped

1 teaspoon fresh thyme leaves or ½ teaspoon dried thyme (but fresh is best)

2 small courgettes/zucchini, sliced

150 g/1 cup cooked peas

2–3 pre-cooked artichoke hearts

1 tablespoon chopped fresh mint

125 g/½ cup kefir cheese

6 eggs

125 ml/½ cup whole milk

sea salt and black pepper, to season

SERVES 4

Using a large, heavy-based frying pan/skillet, heat the oil over medium heat, then add the onion, garlic, thyme and sliced courgettes/zucchini. Cook for 2–3 minutes, until the courgettes/zucchini start to brown. Add the peas, artichoke hearts and mint, and stir together.

Remove the pan from the heat and dollop the kefir cheese on top.

In a bowl, whisk up the eggs with the milk and a pinch each of salt and pepper, then pour over the top of the vegetables and jiggle the pan so the egg mixture reaches the bottom and is evenly spread amongst the vegetables.

Return the pan to low heat and leave it to cook for 3–4 minutes.

Preheat the grill/broiler to hot.

Cook the top of the frittata under the grill/broiler to make sure that the eggs are cooked from the bottom to the top. You'll know it's ready when you poke it with a knife and you can't see any runny egg mixture.

Serve the frittata warm, straight from the pan, or leave it to cool down and serve it cold for a picnic. It's delicious both ways.

NOTE If you can't find pre-cooked artichokes in the deli section at the store, you can always prepare them yourself. Put the fresh artichokes in a saucepan of salted boiling water. Cover with a lid and simmer for 20–30 minutes, depending on the size of the artichokes. Once cooked, the stems will be soft enough to poke a knife through easily. You can then peel the leaves off, eat them along the way, and use just the hearts for this dish.

Ⓑ ASIAN TOFU AND RAW KALE SALAD

This recipe is a plant-based recipe, specifically designed to feed your bones and teeth. Most people know already that calcium is needed for good, strong bones and that milk is most commonly associated with calcium, but what about if you don't eat animal products or you are dairy intolerant? Kale and other dark, leafy green vegetables are an excellent source of calcium, and tofu and soy products are a great natural source of vitamin D. Both are essential for keeping the structure of bones and teeth healthy and keeping osteoporosis at bay. In fact, they work together as vitamin D is needed to help absorb calcium effectively in the body.

a bunch of kale
3 spring onions/
  scallions, finely
  chopped
2 tablespoons chopped
  fresh coriander/
  cilantro
2 tablespoons chopped
  fresh mint
2 tablespoons toasted
  sesame seeds
a block of firm tofu
2 tablespoons vegetable
  oil (optional)
2 tablespoons dried fried
  onions

DRESSING
juice of 1 lime
1 tablespoon fish sauce
  (optional)
1 teaspoon sesame oil
1½ tablespoons olive oil
1 tablespoon finely
  chopped fresh ginger
1 tablespoon honey or
  agave syrup
a pinch each of sea salt
  and black pepper

SERVES 2

To prepare the kale, you need to cut away the stems as these are too hard to digest. Wash all the leaves to get rid of any grit, then fold the leaves together and slice thinly. Put in a large mixing bowl.

Whisk all the dressing ingredients together in a small bowl. Pour two-thirds of the dressing over the kale and massage and squeeze the kale with the dressing using your hands, this helps to soften the kale, making it easier to digest. Leave the kale to sit in the fridge for an hour, or even overnight. Keep the spare dressing for serving.

Toss the kale with the spring onions/scallions, coriander/cilantro, mint and sesame seeds.

Drain the tofu and wrap in a few layers of paper towels. Put something heavy on top (a can of beans or similar) for 10 minutes to help press out any excess water.

You can have the salad with the tofu cold and raw, simply unwrap it and cut into slices to top the salad.

If you prefer it cooked, slice into 1-cm/½-inch thick pieces, add the 2 tablespoons of oil to a frying pan/skillet and set over medium heat. When hot, lay the slices of tofu in the pan. Fry for 2–3 minutes on each side, until it crisps up a bit.

Serve the kale with slices of tofu on top, a drizzle of the leftover dressing and a sprinkle of dried fried onions.

ⒷⓈ HEIRLOOM TOMATO AND SMOKED MACKEREL SALAD WITH CARAMELIZED ONIONS AND GREEK YOGURT DRESSING

Mackerel is an oily fish, full of essential fatty acids and omega-3s, which help keep your joints healthy and flexible. Mackerel is also an excellent source of vitamin D as well as anti-inflammatory compounds, which help ease joint pain.

100 g/2 cups rocket/ arugula
3 heirloom tomatoes, sliced
juice of ½ lemon
a pinch of salt
1 tablespoon olive oil
2 smoked mackerel fillets (I like the peppered fillets)

CARAMELIZED ONIONS
2 tablespoons olive oil
1 large red onion, sliced
1 tablespoon red wine vinegar

GREEK YOGURT DRESSING
115 g/½ cup plain Greek yogurt
1½ tablespoons chopped fresh mint
1 tablespoon chopped fresh flat-leaf parsley
1 garlic clove, finely chopped
¼ cucumber, finely chopped
a pinch each of sea salt and black pepper
1 teaspoon honey
½ teaspoon lemon zest

SERVES 2

Start by making the caramelized onions. Heat the oil in a frying pan/skillet over low heat, add the onion and cook slowly for 10 minutes, stirring every now and then. Once soft and beginning to caramelize, add the vinegar and cook for a further 1 minute. Take off the heat.

Whisk all the ingredients for the dressing together in a small bowl and set aside.

Put the rocket/arugula and tomatoes into a large mixing bowl with the lemon juice, salt and olive oil. Toss to coat everything in oil, then arrange on serving plates.

Break the mackerel up using your hands – this way you can feel for bones and discard any. Arrange the mackerel on top of the salad. Top with the caramelized onions and spoon over the dressing.

Serve immediately.

The recipes in this chapter are designed to be served as an entrée or main course. I always like to keep my recipes simple and easy to prepare so that other people can make them at home too without much fuss. There is a wide range of recipes to try out here, with variety being the key to a well-balanced beauty and health diet. All these dinners are designed to not only taste delicious but to make you more beautiful from the inside out.

Larger plates

D S MISO BAKED SALMON

The omega-3 fatty acids found in salmon have been linked with helping ease inflammatory skin conditions and preventing aging in the body. Omega-3s are good fats that also help protect the skin from sun damage. They contain a wealth of antioxidants to fight free radicals (see page 8) and keep the toxins out, making sure your skin is kept looking smooth and feeling soft! Daikon is a wonderful radish widely used in Asia. One of its many health benefits is that it is a natural diuretic, helping to stimulate your kidneys to flush out toxins from the body.

2 x 200-g/7-oz. fillets of
   fresh salmon
2 tablespoons white miso
   paste
¼ teaspoon white pepper
1 tablespoon honey

PICKLED DAIKON
125 ml/½ cup rice
   vinegar
½ teaspoon sea salt
2 tablespoons white
   sugar
½ small cucumber, sliced
1 fresh red chilli/chile,
   finely chopped
a 10-cm/4-inch piece of
   fresh daikon radish,
   thinly sliced
60 g/½ cup chopped
   pineapple chunks

SERVES 2

Start by preparing the pickled daikon. Heat the rice vinegar, salt and sugar together in a saucepan over low heat until melted. Take off the heat and leave to cool. Put the remaining ingredients in a large mixing bowl and once the vinegar has cooled, pour it over the top. Cover and leave in the fridge to chill while you prepare the salmon. (This pickle can be made up to 3 hours in advance.)

To cook the salmon, lay the fillets on a non-stick baking sheet, skin-side down. Mix together the miso paste, white pepper and honey in a small bowl and smear over the top and around the edge of each salmon fillet. At this point, I like to leave the salmon to marinate at room temperature for at least 30 minutes before cooking, and by that time the pickled daikon should be nicely chilled if you haven't prepared it in advance.

When you are ready to cook, preheat the oven to 220°C (425°F) Gas 7.

Bake the salmon in the preheated oven for 10–12 minutes – the miso will start to caramelize on top and the salmon flesh should be a paler pink colour all the way through, once cooked. If using very fresh salmon, it is fine to leave it slightly undercooked with a darker pink centre (some people prefer it that way) but bake for as long as you like.

To serve, lay the salmon fillets on serving plates. Drain the liquid from the pickled daikon and divide evenly between the plates. This dish is delicious served hot or cold.

s GREEN TEA COCONUT CHICKEN

Matcha green tea powder is a concentrated form of green tea and is best known for being used in Japanese cuisine. It has a wealth of health benefits, but for the skin it is known to be one of the most potent antioxidants that nature has provided – it protects the skin from free radicals, harmful UV rays, and therefore premature aging. The green colour comes from its high chlorophyll content which helps detoxify the body. It is also said to help increase metabolism to burn off calories with greater ease and to boost your energy levels.

I drink a cup of matcha green tea every day and you can even use it in homemade face masks to apply topically to your skin.

2 tablespoons coconut oil
½ onion, finely chopped
450 g/1 lb. chicken
   breast pieces
1–2 teaspoons matcha
   green tea powder, plus
   extra to serve
1 tablespoon honey

about 200 ml/¾ cup
   coconut milk
a pinch each of sea salt
   and white pepper
steamed rice, to serve
toasted flaked/slivered
   almonds, to serve

SERVES 2

Heat the coconut oil in a saucepan over low–medium heat. Add the chopped onion and cook gently for 2–3 minutes until soft. Add the chicken pieces and cook until they are white all over, then stir in the matcha green tea powder, honey and coconut milk. Simmer gently for a further 7–8 minutes, until the chicken is cooked all the way through. If you like more sauce, you can add a dash more coconut milk or a little water to slacken the mixture.

Season the dish with the salt and white pepper and serve, sprinkled with a little extra matcha green tea powder, on a bed of steamed rice with a sprinkle of toasted flaked/slivered almonds on top.

Ⓗ SCALLOPS WITH SAUTÉED MAITAKE MUSHROOMS AND SPINACH

This simple dish doesn't need the addition of heavy sauces or dressings as the ingredients alone are just so delicious by themselves. Scallops, I am very happy to say, are a great source of cystine, which is the amino acid essential for healthy hair, skin, bones and connective tissue. Plus they are my absolute favourite shellfish, so now I have even more of a reason to eat them. The maitake mushroom is a great source of vitamin D and spinach is a good source of biotin and iron, all of which are essential nutrients for strong, shiny hair.

200 g/4 cups spinach
3 tablespoons olive oil
2 tablespoons fresh lemon juice
1 large maitake mushroom or a handful of oyster mushrooms
1 garlic clove, finely chopped
2 teaspoons ghee or butter
6–8 fresh scallops
1 teaspoon lemon zest
sea salt and black pepper, to season

SERVES 2

Start by wilting the spinach in a pan of simmering water, just dunk it all in for 30–45 seconds, then drain. Rinse the spinach with cold water and gently squeeze out any excess water. Put the spinach into a large mixing bowl with 1 tablespoon of the olive oil, 1 tablespoon of the lemon juice and a pinch of salt, and toss together.

Wash the maitake mushroom well to get rid of any soil or grit. Starting from the stem, pull the mushroom apart into 8 pieces. Heat the remaining olive oil in a large frying pan/skillet over medium heat and add the mushroom pieces. Cook for about 2 minutes on each side, depending how big the pieces are, then just before they are nearly cooked, sprinkle over the chopped garlic and a pinch each of salt and pepper, and let the garlic cook with the mushroom pieces until it starts to turn golden, which won't take long.

While the mushrooms are cooking, in a separate pan over medium heat, warm the ghee. Add the scallops and cook for 1–2 minutes on each side, depending on the size – they won't take longer than 2–4 minutes in total in the pan.

To serve, simply arrange everything together on a plate, the spinach, scattered with cooked maitake mushroom pieces, dotted with the scallops in-between. Sprinkle with lemon zest and enjoy.

CHILLI/CHILE AND ORANGE TOFU WITH KALE, BROCCOLI AND BRUSSELS SPROUTS

B **S** **M**

Tofu is recorded in Chinese History for nearly 2,000 years. It's made from curdled soy bean milk and has many health benefits, such as helping with weight loss, symptoms of heart disease and menopause, the effects of skin aging and hair loss. It is high in protein, calcium and vitamin E, low in carbs and has zero cholesterol. You can use it in smoothies, add it to salads, sandwiches and curries (my favourite), or add it to a simple stir-fry. Every Chinese meal my mother ever made always included a tofu dish.

This salad is packed with skin-boosting goodness. Powerful antioxidants, vitamins and minerals from the Brussels sprouts, kale and broccoli, and protein and vitamin E from the tofu to keep skin soft and supple.

½ red onion, thinly sliced

50 g/1 cup broccoli florets

100 g/1 cup Brussels sprouts

100 g/2 cups kale, chopped

1 block firm tofu (about 120 g/4 oz.)

2 tablespoons olive oil

2 tablespoons chopped hazelnuts

steamed brown rice, to serve

CHILLI/CHILE AND ORANGE SAUCE

juice of 1 orange (about 125 ml/½ cup)

2 tablespoons honey

2 tablespoons soy sauce

a 2.5-cm/1-inch piece of ginger, finely chopped

2 garlic cloves, finely chopped

1 fresh red chilli/chile, chopped

1 tablespoon cornflour/cornstarch

SERVES 2

Begin by preparing the chilli/chile and orange sauce. Whisk all of the ingredients together in a small bowl and leave to one side.

Prepare all your vegetables by cutting into small pieces. Drain the tofu and place between a few paper towels with a plate or can on top for 10 minutes to get rid of excess water. Then cut into large chunks.

Set a large frying pan/skillet or wok over medium–high heat and add the olive oil. When hot, carefully add the tofu pieces and stir-fry until they are golden brown all over. Add the onion, broccoli and Brussels sprouts and stir-fry for 2 minutes. Add the kale, sauce and hazelnuts, and stir-fry quickly for another minute, or until the kale has softened slightly.

Serve right away with a side of steamed brown rice.

Tofu

Tofu is a great plant-based source of protein, calcium and vitamin D, which are all essential for strong muscle and bone health. Vitamin D helps the body absorb calcium more easily. Tofu also helps build skin elasticity and keratin for strong, shiny hair. It is low-carb and has low levels of cholesterol.

(M) (H) CHIA CHIMICHURRI STEAK

Protein is the building block for a healthy head of luscious locks and this protein-packed recipe is bursting full of robust and vibrant flavours. The steak is full of iron, and the chia seeds in the sauce are also high in protein, zinc, iron, copper as well as amino acids. Hair needs these nutrients to stay strong and grow long. Copper is also known for keeping the greys at bay!

700 g/1½ lbs. rump or
sirloin beef steak

DRESSING
125 g/1¼ cups fresh
flat-leaf parsley
125 g/1¼ cups fresh
coriander/cilantro
a small handful of fresh
basil
125 ml/½ cup olive oil
2 tablespoons chia seeds
2 small shallots, peeled

2 fresh serrano peppers
or jalapeños
3–4 garlic cloves, peeled
2 tablespoons cider
vinegar or red wine
vinegar
juice of 1 lime
½ teaspoon sea salt

a food processor

SERVES 4–6

Simply add all of the dressing ingredients to a food processor and whizz to a fairly fine consistency – it doesn't have to be completely finely ground, I like mine to keep a little texture.

To marinate the steak, smear a couple of tablespoons of the dressing over the steak and rub all over. Leave for at least 30 minutes but ideally a couple of hours. If leaving for longer, refrigerate and then remove from the fridge 30 minutes before cooking to allow it to come to room temperature.

Cook the steak to your liking, either on a barbecue grill or a griddle pan over medium–high heat. Leave the steak to rest once cooked, then slice to serve.

Mix a couple of tablespoons of the remaining dressing with an extra 1 tablespoon of olive oil to make it runnier, and drizzle over the top of the steak, or serve the extra dressing on the side.

Any leftover dressing can be kept in an airtight container in the fridge for up to 1 week.

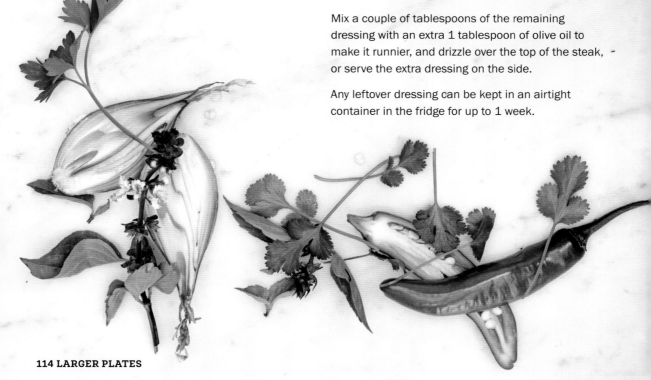

Ⓔ STEAK, SEAWEED AND SOBA NOODLES

Seaweed and other water plants like kelp are highly nutritious. They contain large amounts of vitamin A, which is needed for good eyesight, can help to prevent dry eyes and night blindness, and generally improves your vision.

Seaweed is also a great source of magnesium which is essential to eye health. It relaxes the eye muscles, helping to prevent twitching of the eyes and even ocular migraines. Magnesium also helps prevent too much calcium being absorbed into the body, which can lead to cloudy cataracts.

Once you buy a packet of dried seaweed, you'll have it on hand to rehydrate at your convenience and add it to as many things as you like! It's packed full of so many good nutrients that I love to add a little sprinkling of seaweed to many dishes, including salads and even my green smoothies!

200 g/7 oz. dried soba noodles

2 tablespoons dried seaweed

2 tablespoons algae oil or oil of your choice

2 teaspoons sesame oil

3 big garlic cloves, finely chopped

a 225-g/8-oz. sirloin steak, sliced into strips

5 spring onions/ scallions, thinly sliced lengthways

1 teaspoon sesame seeds

DRESSING

3 tablespoons dark soy sauce

1 tablespoon honey

½ teaspoon white pepper

SERVES 2

Start by preparing the noodles. Put a large saucepan of water over medium heat and bring to the boil. When the water is boiling, add the noodles and simmer for 3–4 minutes, until just soft. Drain and rinse the noodles quickly under cold running water to stop further cooking. Set aside.

While the noodles are cooking, put the seaweed into a medium mixing bowl and pour over 500 ml/2 cups of water. Set aside to rehydrate for 10 minutes – the seaweed will expand and soak up some of the water. Drain off any excess water.

Whisk together the soy sauce, honey and pepper for the dressing in a small bowl.

Now you are ready to stir-fry!

Heat the algae and sesame oils together in a wok set over medium–high heat. When the wok is hot and almost smoking, add the garlic, then the steak and spring onions/scallions, and stir-fry for about 1 minute. Once the steak is browned all over, add the rehydrated seaweed and stir-fry together for another 15 seconds, then add in the cooked noodles and the dressing. Quickly stir everything together and keep the wok on the heat for another 30 seconds to make sure all the sauce is absorbed by the noodles.

Serve steaming-hot, straight from the wok, with a sprinkle of sesame seeds on top.

M TURKEY CHILLI WITH CHOCOLATE, MOLASSES AND BLACK BEANS

I love this dish on a cool evening and use ground turkey to make it lower in fat than chilli con carne made with ground beef, but still high in protein – the building blocks of your muscles. The added magic is the dark/bittersweet chocolate and molasses, which turn it into a deep, rich and heart-warming dish. Pure dark/bittersweet chocolate made with 100 per cent cocoa solids has many incredible health benefits. A recent study discovered a component in chocolate that helps to keep your arteries flexible and less prone to clogging. Black strap molasses have the lowest sugar content of all cane sugar products and they are packed full of important minerals and vitamins, including iron, which battles fatigue and improves endurance and power.

2 tablespoons olive oil
1 onion, chopped
3 garlic cloves, finely chopped
1 red (bell) pepper, deseeded and chopped
1 teaspoon smoked paprika
1 teaspoon ground cumin
1 teaspoon dried oregano
450 g/1 lb. ground turkey
a 420-g/15-oz. can of black beans, drained and rinsed
a 400-g/14-oz. can of chopped tomatoes
500 ml/2 cups chicken stock
2 tablespoons black strap molasses
2 tablespoons chopped dark/bittersweet chocolate
a pinch each of sea salt and black pepper, to season

TO SERVE (OPTIONAL)
steamed brown rice
1 avocado, flesh cut into pieces
1 spring onion/scallion, thinly sliced
a pinch of smoked dried chilli/red pepper flakes
1 lime, cut into wedges
fresh coriander/cilantro leaves

SERVES 4

Heat the olive oil in a large, deep pan or pot over medium heat. Add the onion, garlic, (bell) pepper, paprika, cumin and oregano. Cook for a couple of minutes until the onion and pepper are soft. Add the turkey and cook for a further 3–4 minutes until the turkey has turned white. Add the beans, tomatoes, stock and molasses. Bring the mixture to the boil, then turn the heat down to a simmer, cover the pan with a lid (but slightly ajar) and leave to cook for 40 minutes. Stir in the chocolate, season with salt and pepper and serve piping hot with steamed brown rice and a variety of toppings, if you like.

This dish also tastes great the next day, so it's a good one to make in advance if you have people over. I also freeze mine in individual portions ready to thaw and reheat another time.

Turkey

White turkey meat is one of the leanest sources of animal protein out there. Protein is used in every cell in our bodies. It is used to help build and repair tissues, to make enzymes and hormones, and is the building block of bones, muscles, cartilage, skin and blood.

BUTTERNUT SQUASH, GREEN BEAN AND ENOKI THAI COCONUT CURRY

E S D

This simple curry uses a host of natural beauty ingredients in one dish. Butternut squash is a great source of beta-carotene, which converts to vitamin A in our bodies for healthy eyes, skin and a strong immune system. The coconut milk is full of moisturizing fatty acids and the black rice is packed full of fibre, antioxidant anthocyanin and a good amount of vitamin E, which helps prevent aging. Plus it's naturally gluten-free.

400 g/2 cups black rice
½ onion, chopped
2 tablespoons grated fresh ginger
2 lemongrass stalks, outer leaves removed
2 garlic cloves
20 g/½ cup fresh coriander/cilantro, plus extra to garnish
1 tablespoon coconut oil
1½ tablespoons Thai red curry paste
250 g/2 cups diced butternut squash
a pinch each of sea salt and black pepper
1 teaspoon honey
125 ml/½ cup coconut milk
140 g/1 cup halved green/French beans
a bunch of enoki mushrooms, washed and torn into chunks

SERVES 4

The black rice takes longer to cook than the curry so start with this. Put the rice and 1 litre/4 cups of water into a large saucepan with a lid. Bring to the boil over medium heat, then turn the heat down to its lowest setting. Pop the lid on and cook for 40 minutes. Turn off the heat, give it a stir and leave the lid on for a further 10 minutes.

Meanwhile, blend the onion, ginger, lemongrass garlic and coriander/cilantro in a food processor.

Put a large saucepan over medium heat, add the coconut oil and then the ground onion mixture and Thai red curry paste. Cook for 1–2 minutes stirring all the time. Add the butternut squash, 500 ml/ 2 cups of water, the salt, pepper and honey, and leave to simmer gently for 10–12 minutes, until the squash is nearly soft through. Add the coconut milk, green/French beans and enoki mushrooms and simmer for a further 6–7 minutes.

Serve the curry on a bed of steaming hot black rice with fresh coriander/cilantro on top.

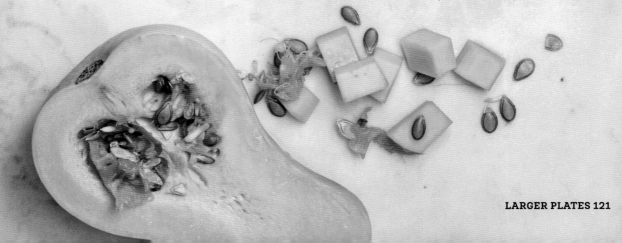

(M) D HIGH-FIBRE CHICKEN TAGINE

I love to find ways of adding extra goodness to my dishes while keeping the flavours well-balanced. Adding chickpeas to this tagine is a perfect example. Chickpeas are known for their high fibre content. In relation to digestive health, a large part of the fibre in them is insoluble fibre that travels to your large intestine without being digested. It is then metabolized to support cell health and keep the colon healthy. You don't need a tagine to follow this recipe, but if you have one, great! If you don't, you can use a large frying pan/skillet with a lid. The bitter lemon, salty olives and sweet onions and spices make this a truly delicious and different way to cook up a simple chicken dinner.

3 tablespoons olive oil
1 large red onion, sliced
3 garlic cloves, finely chopped
2 teaspoons ground ginger
¼ teaspoon ground cardamom
1 teaspoon ground cinnamon
1 small preserved lemon, finely chopped
juice of ½ lemon
450 g/1 lb. chicken thighs, cut in half (about 6 thighs)
115 g/scant 1 cup cooked chickpeas
100 g/1 cup pitted/ stoned purple olives
3 tablespoons chopped fresh flat-leaf parsley
3 tablespoons chopped fresh coriander/ cilantro, plus extra leaves to garnish
a pinch of sea salt
200 ml/¾ cup chicken stock
couscous, pitta breads or steamed brown rice, to serve

SERVES 4

Heat the olive oil in a deep frying pan/skillet with a lid or tagine with a heat diffuser (if you have one) over low heat. Add the onion, garlic and all the spices: ginger, cardamom and cinnamon. Sprinkle the preserved lemon into the pan, then add the lemon juice. I let this gently cook together for 7–8 minutes to caramelize the onions.

Lay the chicken thighs on top, then the chickpeas and olives, followed by the chopped herbs and a pinch of salt. Pour the chicken stock over the top and push the chicken down a bit so it is just about covered. Pop a lid on the pan or tagine and leave to simmer for 35–40 minutes. The sauce will be lovely and thick and the chicken cooked through after this time.

Garnish with coriander/cilantro and serve with either couscous, pitta breads or even a bowl of steamed brown rice.

Ginger

Ginger has been used in China and Asia for medicinal purposes for many centuries. The bioactive ingredient is called gingerol, which has powerful antioxidant and anti-inflammatory effects. It's widely known to help ease the feeling of nausea and to help fight infections.

WILD MUSHROOM FARRO RISOTTO

Mushrooms have been widely used in Far Eastern cultures for their medicinal and immune-boosting properties for centuries. My mother always had cupboards full of strange-shaped dried mushrooms, which she would add to any number of soups and stocks. The ancient Romans named them the 'Gifts of the Gods'. Mushrooms have an array of beneficial nutrients, but the three that stand out as being best for your bones are copper, zinc and selenium. Shiitake mushrooms have the highest amount of copper, but all mushrooms contain a good supply of the mineral. Copper is needed by the body to help produce connective tissues, elastin and collagen. It is therefore important for keeping bones and joints supple and healthy. Some scientific studies have linked selenium deficiency with osteoporosis.

75 g/½ cup farro, soaked in water overnight

1 tablespoon ghee or butter

2 garlic cloves, finely chopped

125 ml/½ cup white wine

500 ml/2 cups warm vegetable stock

10 g/½ cup dried porcini mushrooms, soaked in 375 ml/1½ cups hot water

60 g/2 cups sliced fresh shiitake mushrooms or a mixture of fresh mushrooms

2 tablespoons grated Parmesan cheese

SERVES 2

NOTE Farro cooks quicker when it has been soaked overnight first.

Heat the ghee on a medium to low heat in a large saucepan, add the garlic and farro grains and stir to coat. Slowly add the white wine a bit at a time and keep stirring until all the liquid is used up. Do the same for the vegetable stock and lastly the porcini water, along with the porcini mushrooms, and sliced mushrooms towards the end. The trick with a risotto is to cook it slowly; the process will take about 30 minutes of adding liquid and stirring.

Once it's cooked most of the liquid will be absorbed, but there should still be some left so make sure it's not completely dry, if it is add a little more stock.

Lastly, stir in the Parmesan cheese and serve hot. The farro should still be slightly chewy with a little bite to it. It adds a lovely, nutty flavour to the risotto.

The perfect way to finish a great meal is to have a little something sweet. Desserts and treats do not have to be full of ingredients that are bad for you to taste good. Mother Nature has kindly supplied us with a gorgeous selection of sweet ingredients, like cocoa, berries, fruits, nuts, honey and some delicious grains to make a wealth of recipes that satisfy the sweet tooth and that also make us shine.

Desserts and treats

ⓈⒿ BLUEBERRY AND COCONUT CRUMBLE POTS

Blueberries and coconuts together have enough antioxidants and essential fats to keep skin plump and moisturized. Blueberries contain phytochemicals, which help neutralize free radicals that damage our skin cells. The high level of vitamin C in the blueberries helps to keep our blood vessels strong to prevent any breakage leading to spider veins. They are also a good source of vitamin A, which is widely used in the treatment of acne.

65 g/½ cup spelt flour
40 g/½ cup desiccated/ shredded or flaked coconut
4 tablespoons ghee
2–3 tablespoons palm sugar or raw brown sugar
a pinch of sea salt
1 tablespoon cornflour/ cornstarch
2 tablespoons chia seeds
35 g/¼ cup pumpkin seeds
70 g/½ cup old-fashioned rolled oats

BLUEBERRY FILLING
300 g/2½ cups fresh or frozen blueberries
1–2 tablespoons raw demerara/turbinado sugar
zest of 1 lemon
1 teaspoon cornflour/ cornstarch

a food processor (optional)
a baking sheet lined with baking parchment

SERVES 4

Preheat the oven to 180°C (350°F) Gas 4.

I make the crumble topping in a food processor because I find it easier, quicker and the mixture comes out great, but you could work everything together by hand in a large mixing bowl.

Put the spelt flour, coconut, ghee, sugar, salt and cornflour/cornstarch into a food processor and pulse to form breadcrumbs. Transfer to a large mixing bowl and add the chia seeds, pumpkin seeds and oats. Stir together – it will now be forming clumps so squish it together a bit with your hands, then spread the crumble onto the prepared baking sheet.

Bake in the preheated oven for 15–20 minutes, until it is cooked, crisp and golden.

While the crumble is cooking, prepare the blueberry filling. Put the blueberries, sugar and lemon zest into a saucepan with 1 tablespoon of water. Bring to the boil, then simmer until the blueberries pop open – this should only take a couple of minutes.

In a small bowl, mix the cornflour/cornstarch with 1 tablespoon of water, then stir into the blueberries. Keep stirring until the sauce thickens, then remove the pan from the heat.

Divide the filling between your serving pots, and sprinkle the crumble over the top. Serve up hot.

SUPER FRUIT AND NUT CHOCOLATE BRITTLE

S
M

Forget what you may have heard about chocolate ruining your skin. Dark/bittersweet chocolate with a high cocoa solids content of at least 70 per cent contains flavonoids that protect the skin from harmful UV rays. Add coconut to the mix with this brittle and you'll have the added bonus of introducing cytokinins to your body, which are said to be anti-aging. This crunchy and hard brittle is a delicious and healthy sweet treat.

200 g/1½ cups mixed nuts, chopped (I like brazil nuts, pistachios, almonds and hazelnuts)

75 g/1 cup dessicated/ shredded or flaked coconut

200 g/7 oz. dark/ bittersweet chocolate (70 per cent cocoa solids)

3 tablespoons agave syrup or honey

75 g/½ cup mixed dried super berries (I like goji, inca/ golden, cranberries, blueberries, tart cherries)

a baking sheet lined with baking parchment

SERVES 6–8

Preheat the oven to 180°C (350°F) Gas 4.

Spread the nuts onto an unlined baking sheet along with the coconut. Pop into the preheated oven to toast for 5 minutes, until you can see the coconut turning golden – it will smell amazing! Remove from the oven and set aside to cool.

Break the chocolate into small pieces and pop into a heatproof bowl with the agave syrup. Set the bowl over a pan of barely simmering water and stir to melt.

Transfer the cooled nuts to a large mixing bowl, add the super berries and pour in the melted chocolate. Mix together well, then spread the mixture onto the prepared baking sheet. Spread the mixture quite thinly as you want the consistency to be like chocolate brittle rather than a chocolate bar.

Put the baking sheet in the fridge to harden the chocolate for 1 hour. After this time, you can take it out and break it up or cut it into bite-size pieces.

Store in an airtight container in the fridge for up to 2 weeks.

ⓢ VEGAN CHOCOLATE AND AVOCADO TRUFFLES

Firstly, you wouldn't even know these creamy, decadent chocolate truffles were vegan! Secondly, they are full of nutrients to keep your skin glowing from the inside out. The antioxidants found in good-quality dark/bittersweet chocolate can protect the skin from free radicals. Whenever I write about free radicals and skin damage, I have an image in my head of a potential war going on inside my body – the free radicals are terrorizing my healthy cells and need to be stopped by the antioxidant army, the hero of youth and vitality. Combined with the high levels of vitamin E and oleic acid in avocado, these truffles give the skin a beauty boost. Oleic acid is a monounsaturated fatty acid which helps keep the epidermal layer of the skin moist, soft and hydrated.

280 g/10 oz. vegan dark/bittersweet chocolate (70 per cent cocoa solids)
1 ripe avocado
a pinch of sea salt
½ teaspoon vanilla extract
1 tablespoon agave syrup or caster/granulated sugar

COATINGS (CHOOSE ONE OF THE BELOW OR A MIXTURE OF ALL)
desiccated/shredded coconut
chopped pistachios
chopped flaked/slivered almonds
chopped hazelnuts
cocoa powder

MAKES 20

Break the chocolate into small pieces and pop into a heatproof bowl. Set the bowl over a pan of barely simmering water and stir to melt. Once melted, stir in the agave syrup or sugar. Set aside to cool slightly.

Scoop the avocado flesh into a large mixing bowl, discarding the pip/stone, add the salt and mash it to a very fine pulp.

Add the avocado to the cooled melted chocolate with the vanilla and gently fold together. Pop the mixture in the fridge to set for 30 minutes, or until much more firm. Meanwhile, put the coatings in shallow bowls.

Next, roll the chocolate mixture into balls. Scoop a small tablespoon into the palms of your hands and quickly roll it into a ball, then immediately roll in whichever coating you want.

Continue until you have used up all the chocolate mixture. Put the truffles in an airtight container and chill for at least 30 minutes before serving. Store in the fridge and eat within 2 days.

Chocolate

The flavanols in dark/bittersweet chocolate are a type of flavonoid (antioxidant), which help keep the skin protected from free radicals and sun damage, and improves blood flow to the skin, keeping skin plump and wrinkle-free. But my favourite benefit of dark/bittersweet chocolate is that it helps reduce stress hormones. Stress has a terrible effect on our bodies in many different ways, but for the skin, it causes a reduced production of collagen, which reduces fine lines.

S D BLACK RICE COCONUT PUDDING

This is a Malaysian dish, made with a sticky black rice grain, called 'bubur pulut hitam'. I grew up on desserts like this, consisting of rice, coconut and palm sugar. The pandan leaf is a long, green leaf commonly used to flavour desserts and sweet treats in Asia. I call it 'the Asian vanilla'. The dark colour of the rice indicates that it is full of anthocyanins, which are powerful, natural antioxidants, and they produce the dark purple 'black' flavonoid colour in foods such as grapes, rice and berries. The rice is also a great source of fibre, which helps keep your digestive tract healthy by binding to toxins and waste and clearing them out.

140 g/¾ cup black glutinous rice, soaked in water for 30 minutes or overnight

2 pandan leaves or 1 teaspoon vanilla extract

90 g/½ cup palm sugar or raw brown sugar

125 ml/½ cup coconut milk

toasted dessicated/ shredded and flaked coconut, to serve

Drain the soaked rice and transfer to a saucepan. Pour over 1.25 litres/5 cups of water and bring to the boil. Tie the pandan leaves in a knot and add into the rice (or add the vanilla extract). Cover with a lid, turn down the heat and simmer for about 40 minutes, giving it a stir every now and then to make sure nothing is sticking.

Once the rice has cooked down, is soft and nearly all the water has evaporated, it is done! You can add more water if you prefer it runnier.

Stir in the sugar and serve with the coconut milk and toasted coconut.

SERVES 4

B PINEAPPLE AND MINT CRUSH

Pineapple has to be one of my favourite tropical fruits, and it has so many good vitamins and minerals. It is a great natural source of manganese, which is a trace mineral needed by our bodies to build strong bones and connective tissue. The bromelain found in pineapples has also been found to help with osteoarthritis by relieving painful joints with its anti-inflammatory properties.

1 small ripe pineapple
zest and juice of 1 lime
20 g/½ cup fresh mint, finely chopped
3 tablespoons/⅓ cup palm sugar or raw brown sugar

2 tablespoons dark rum (optional)

SERVES 4

Peel, core and chop the whole pineapple into small bite-size cubes and put in a large serving bowl. (You can also buy prepared and cut fresh pineapple to save time.) Pour the lime juice over the top.

Put the chopped mint in a separate small bowl, add the sugar and lime zest and smoosh together with the back of a spoon. (You can use a pestle and mortar if you have one.)

Sprinkle the mint mixture over the pineapple, mix together and serve straight away so the sugar still has a little crunch when you eat it.

I love serving this dish as a refreshing dessert on a hot day at a BBQ – if it's just grown-ups, then add a dash of rum in there too – it goes down very well.

BERRY AND BAOBAB ANTIOXIDANT BALLS

D
S

This is an afternoon pick-me-up that your face will love! Plus, after making these little balls of beauty heaven, you'll feel like you've also had a moisturizing hand treatment. Goji berries have been used in Chinese medicine for thousands of years. They are particularly good for your skin, and, as well as the blueberries and baobab, they contain high levels of anti-oxidants and vitamin C.

130 g/1 cup almonds or
   cashews
a pinch of sea salt
50 g/½ cup goji berries
85 g/½ cup dried wild
   blueberries
4 dates, stoned/pitted
1 tablespoon baobab
   fruit powder

1 tablespoon virgin
   coconut oil
20 g/¼ cup desiccated/
   shredded coconut

a food processor

SERVES 4

Start by putting the nuts and salt into a food processor. Blitz until they are chunky but not finely ground, then add the berries, dates, baobab fruit powder and coconut oil, and blitz until the mixture starts clumping together – it doesn't have to be puréed or too finely ground, you still want bits.

Roll the mixture into balls with your hands – your hands will feel very soft after making these with the coconut oil in them! Roll each ball in the coconut to coat and enjoy.

Store these balls in an airtight container in the fridge for 3–4 weeks. They can also be frozen for up to 3 months, simply defrost before serving.

IRON-RICH APRICOT AND CASHEW POWER BARS

H
M

Dried apricots are a great source of iron and so they are perfect for women's health especially. Iron deficiency is the most common nutrient deficiency in women, which can lead to a host of ailments such as fatigue, poor concentration and irritability. Iron plays a key role in keeping hair strong and healthy, too, as it carryies oxygen to the hair roots as blood circulates around the body.

30 g/2 tablespoons
   sunflower seeds
115 g/½ cup cashews
30 g/½ cup desiccated/
   shredded coconut
200 g/1 cup dried
   apricots
1½ tablespoons
   crystallized ginger

1 tablespoon virgin
   coconut oil
2 tablespoons agave
   syrup or honey

a food processor
*a square or rectangular
   baking pan lined with
   baking parchment*

MAKES 6

Preheat the oven to 180°C (350°F) Gas 4.

Spread the sunflower seeds, cashews and coconut onto an unlined baking sheet and pop in the preheated oven to toast for 5–6 minutes, or until lightly brown – the coconut will turn faster than the rest, so be careful not to leave it in there too long! Remove from the oven and leave to cool down. Once cool, transfer to a food processor and pulse until finely ground. Tip out into a mixing bowl.

Put the apricots, ginger, coconut oil and agave syrup into the food processor and blitz until almost smooth. Add this mixture to the seed and nut mixture and stir everything together.

Press the mixture firmly into the prepared baking pan, cover with clingfilm/plastic wrap and put in the fridge to chill and harden for at least 1 hour.

Cut the hardened mixture into bars, enjoy or store in an airtight container in the fridge for up to 2 weeks.

INDEX

SUPPLIERS

Amazing Grass
www.amazinggrass.com
A great source of green superfoods, such as wheatgrass.

Amazon
www.amazon.co.uk
www.amazon.com
An online retailer of everything you need to prepare beauty foods.

Borough Market
www.boroughmarket.org.uk
Central London food market.

Eataly
www.eataly.com
UK and US retailer of good-quality ingredients from the deli counter and fridge.

Farmers' Markets
www.farma.org.uk (UK)
www.ams.usda.gov (US)
I like to head to farmers' markets as often as possible to buy my fruit, vegetables and local produce. You know the quality is good and the produce is super fresh, plus you're helping support local farmers, too. Visit the FARMA (UK) or AMS (US) websites to find your nearest location.

Holland & Barrett
www.hollandandbarrett.com
UK-based health food retailer with a wide range of products, including dried fruits, nuts, seeds and superfood powders, as well as all-natural cosmetics.

Local Harvest
www.localharvest.org/farmers-markets
Californian directory of local food producers.

Navitas Naturals
www.navitasnaturals.com
I buy a lot of my superfoods from Navitas. Their products are available in Wholefoods Market stores and online.

Planet Organic
www.planetorganic.com
A one-stop shop in the UK for good-quality, organic produce.

Real Foods
www.realfoods.co.uk
Natural foods importer to the US.

Sous Chef
www.souschef.co.uk
For hard-to-find ingredients, including edible flowers.

Thrive Market
www.thrivemarket.com
Whole foods at discounted prices, delivered straight to your door!

True Foods Market
www.truefoodsmarket.com
Supplier of ethically sourced, organic produce in the US.

Wholefoods Market
www.wholefoodsmarket.com
Stockists of everything you need for all of the recipes in this book, available to buy online or in store.

ACKNOWLEDGMENTS

Firstly, I want to acknowledge what a great privilege it is to have the opportunity to write these recipes and to have them published.

I'd like to thank my beautiful late mother whose deep understanding and knowledge of natural beauty shall always be bestowed in me, and who will always be in my heart. Many of her beauty tips shall live on and be passed to you all within the pages of this book. To my beautiful daughter Bethany, as without you I would never have had the courage and determination to get to where I am today. Your natural beauty shines the most from your kind and loving heart, and I hope you will use these recipes yourself and pass them on to your own children. To my late father, whose love of food inspired me from a very young age. To the rest of my family, my sisters and brother, Rose, Michelle and Alex, and to my step-father Michael, thank you for all your help over the years since having my daughter. I couldn't have accomplished all I have so far without all of your loving support.

Thank you to Stephanie Milner at Ryland Peters & Small for thinking of me to write this book, and to all I have had the pleasure of working with there. Thanks to the team who made the book come to life so beautifully, food stylists George Dolese and Elisabet der Nederlanden, photographer Ed Anderson and prop stylist Emma Star Jensen.

To my book agent Alan Nevins. To my manager Suzanne de Passe, whose love and knowledge of food and health is mindblowing, and who is a huge inspiration.

Lastly, to all my friends and loyal subscribers, a massive thank you for always being there and supporting me. I can't tell you how happy and proud I am that after all these years of cooking my first book is being published. This is a special one for you all and I'm glad my recipes will keep you all looking even more beautiful and shining from the inside out.

Thank you for buying this book, I truly hope you enjoy my recipes and that they help keep you strong, healthy and beautiful.